# TO SERVE MY COUNTRY

Jenna Turnipseed

"To Serve My Country," by Jenna Turnipseed. ISBN 978–1-60264–354–3.

Published 2009 by Virtualbookworm.com Publishing Inc., P.O. Box 9949, College Station, TX 77842, US. ©2009, Jenna Turnipseed. All rights reserved.

Manufactured in the United States of America.

For Georgia

# Introduction

I'M A MEMBER OF THE United States Army. I began to write this in the face of deployment. I started writing it a few weeks before we left and continued to write it while I was stationed in Iraq. This book is about me, about the Army, and about why I do what I do. It's to help people understand what my life is like, and the lives of others like me. I'm not a writer and, to tell you the truth, I wasn't even very good at English in high school. But I wanted to give the rest of the world an idea of just what it's like to be a soldier and the wife of a soldier.

# About Me

MY NAME IS JENNA TURNIPSEED. I'm a wife, a mother, and a soldier. I'm 23 years old, from Coos Bay, Oregon, and I'm preparing to go to Iraq. No I'm not complaining. I volunteered. Actually, I've been volunteering for years.

Every time I hear a unit is being deployed, I'm one of the first to put my name on the list. But it always seems that something happens. For example, the unit isn't taking females, or I have the wrong Military Occupation Specialty or MOS. Once, I had to take my name off the list because my husband got in an accident and I had to move. And another time I got pregnant.

I've been in the Army for about six years; seven by the time this deployment is over. I served the first three on active duty, stationed at Fort Hood. Then the next three in the National Guard, where I went from Tennessee to Oregon then Wyoming, and now back to Tennessee again. For about nine months in the middle I was in the IRR (Inactive Ready Reserve) but was working in Iraq as a civilian contractor for most of that time. Which simply means that most all I've known in my adult life has been the Army.

Currently I am a member of the 230th Sustainment Brigade out of Chattanooga, Tennessee. I have been in the unit for about nine months, but I'll be deploying with the 1–181 Field Artillery Battalion, which is another unit that falls under my current brigade.

When I went to drill last month and heard that they had been called up, I immediately volunteered to go with them.

At first, it was questionable whether or not I would get to go. The unit was field artillery, which means no girls and, well, I'm a female. Luckily, as it turned out, the mission is for detainee ops, which enabled me to go with them. So now, after years of waiting to be deployed, I am finally getting to go.

# How It Began

I GREW UP IN A small town on the Southern Oregon coast, called Coos Bay. I can remember back to middle school when I got a pair of jungle boots at the surplus store and wore them around everywhere, earning the nick name G.I. Jane from my wood shop teacher. It wasn't so much because of my attitude or because I was dead set to be in the military. It was mainly just because it was my wardrobe.

My family was big into the Salvation Army. I mean, where else could you go and get a bag full of clothes for three dollars? First, I wore hippy clothes. From there, I started to get into wearing the old solid green army shirts. I loved them. They were vintage, OD green (which looks great on me), and, best of all, they were fifty cents a shirt. Then I went to a surplus store one day and found "the boots." They were the black and green jungle boots. I was so proud of them because I bought them myself. They cost me sixteen dollars. And, after that, they never left my feet. I even wore them to my PE classes when we went running.

Between junior high and high school I changed a little. I went from big shirts to big pants. Most of high school I was somewhere between a skater and a punker, minus the traditional ditch-class-and-do-drugs aspect. I never really did my homework. But I did always go to class. I often slept through it, only staying awake if I was talking or eating. I would find a way to work the grading system so as to do the littlest amount possible and still pass.

I never had good grades. I believe my average freshman year was a 1.2 GPA (I learned early on a D is still passing). But near the end of my freshman year I decided that I wanted to graduate early. So I submitted a plan to the counselor and, in the fall of the next year, I began to take extra classes in the morning at the high school and, at night, at the local community college.

The first college class I ever took was Introduction to Business. At the time I wanted to be a CEO for a major firm. It is the reason I used for wanting to graduate early. I was the youngest person in my business class by ten years, and younger then some by twenty to thirty years. I got a B in the class and, after that the stigma of school wasn't so bad.

I stayed in my classes, and I graduated high school at sixteen. After that, I spent a year working and continuing to go to the local community college. By this time, I had lost interest in being a large corporate executive and had no idea what I wanted to be; just that I wanted to be something.

I thought about being a dancer or going to school for automotive repair, but the idea of how much college cost got to me. Even though my mother offered to help me out, we didn't grow up with a lot of money and it just seemed too much to ask for at the time.

In high school, I had always thought about joining the military but I was always too young. I graduated high school at sixteen so, my senior year, when all the recruiters were giving their presentations in class, I would think about how cool the military could be, but never bothered to really listen or ask any questions. I figured, if I couldn't join, what was the point.

Then one night, in the Spring of my freshman year of college, I was sitting in my car with my boyfriend, Tim, outside his apartment. It was no different than any other night. Since we had started in high school, it had become routine for me to drive him home and then spend hours in the driveway talking. But that night, out of nowhere, I just looked at him and said I was going to join the Army.

I started going off about how it could help me pay for my school and get out on my own. My mind was going a million miles an hour with ideas about it and how good it would be for me. I was so excited that, when I went home that night, I woke my mom up and had to tell her all about this "stellar" plan I had. The next day I was in the recruiter's office.

From day one, I told everyone Army. But I had originally wanted to join the Marines. I had a buddy that was a Marine, and I liked the thought of being the best of the best. I was one of those people who probably would have joined the Marines for no pay and no benefits, just food, water, and shelter. I had known the Marine recruiter for a while, and I was excited to show up in his office that day and tell him I was finally going to join. But as luck had it, he wasn't there. He went on leave and another recruiter was filling in for him. When I walked into the office the recruiter was rude and had a very anti-female attitude. My natural response was, *fine, then I'll go next door*. And so I did.

It just so happened that the Army office was next door. I walked right into the Army office. Sitting behind the door was SFC Garcia, who I had known since high school. He had been my school's Army recruiter for several years. He talked to me for a minute, gave me my paperwork to fill out and, by the end of the meeting, I was on my way to enlisting. I still had to finish the semester I was in at college, but within about two and a half months of walking into the recruiters office I was off to training and on my way to becoming a soldier.

I had joined the military with the thought that it would be a way for me to get off on my own and pay for college; that it would help me decide what I wanted to do with my life and become something. But it turned out to be so much more. It instilled in me a sense of pride and accomplishment that I had

7

never felt. I knew that I was a part of something larger then myself, and I had found my purpose.

# Basic Training

IT WAS THE END OF March when I originally swore in and signed my name on the dotted line. I was supposed to ship on the 28th of June, but I couldn't wait to leave. I persuaded my teachers to let me take my finals early and, on the 6th of June, 2001, I shipped out for basic training.

I'll never forget that day. My great grandfather was at Saint Catherine's, a nursing home with a medical facility on the lower level. He had been there for a while because of cancer, for which he was receiving treatment. He had lost all his hair due to the treatments, and, one day when I went to visit him, I made a joke about shaving my head to look like him. He was a bit older and failed to realize that my comments were in jest. He thought I was serious and, from then on, every day I walked in he made a comment about me shaving my head. He even brought it up to my brother and mother when they went to visit them.

I had just played it off at first, thinking that he would smile and forget about it. I had a ballet recital before I left and really didn't think bald would be a good look for it. Then, the same day I shipped, I went to visit him, and the last thing he said to me was, "Send me a picture of you in your uniform with that bald head."

I realized then he wasn't going to forget and, that night, when I got to the processing station, otherwise known as MEPS, I shaved my head. It took me a second to talk myself into it, but eventually I did. A girl who was staying in my room walked around with me trying to find a barber shop or salon to get it cut, but we couldn't find any. Instead we ended up going across the street to a K-Mart to purchase a pair of scissors and a pack of razors. We went back to the hotel, I put my long hair up into a pony tail and, then, took the scissors and cut the whole thing off. After that, I had to cut all my hair down short enough to shave. I actually had the process down, because I had shaved off most of it a few years back. The whole process took three hours, a pair of scissors, and four Bic razors.

When I showed up at Fort Leonardwood, Missouri for reception, I stuck out like a sore thumb. I was made to walk around with my hands on my head when I was outside. They said it was so it didn't burn. But all the guys were bald, too, and I was the only one they made do it.

On the second day I was there, I actually got yelled out for being in line with the females. A drill sergeant came from the other end of the chow hall, yelling at the top of his lungs, asking me what I was doing in the line with females. I was almost positive he was talking to me, but he was referring to me as a male so I never turned around. When he got all the way to me, he finally realized I was a female, he continued to go off on me about my choice of "haircut." I knew then it was going to be a long nine weeks.

When I got to my basic training unit, it was the same. First the comments came from my drill sergeants, then from the reserve drill sergeants that changed out every two weeks. I ended up getting smoked more than anyone else because I was the easiest to pick out when someone needed a battle buddy.

*Smoked* is a term we used when you were made to do pushups and other exercises as means of corrective training. Whenever somebody does something wrong or says something out of order, that's how they're corrected. It is a way of both inflicting punishment and getting people in shape.

I began to get smoked so much I didn't really mind it. Sometimes it beat sitting through the classes. Some may find it terrible, but I went in the Army with the ability to do three pushups. After nine weeks of getting smoked, I left maxing out that segment of my physical fitness test. The only thing bad about it was that you were never smoked alone. If you did something wrong, you and your battle buddy, another soldier, were smoked together. An attempt to avoid this is what led to my most unforgettable memory; the time I peed my pants in formation. Yes, that's what I said; the time

I peed my pants.

We were only able to use the latrine at specified break times, but we drank a canteen of water every hour in order to hydrate ourselves for the heat. One, day we had an exceptionally long period between breaks. I remember sitting my legs crossed trying to hold it in, knowing that if I got up and used the bathroom I was getting someone else smoked.

Finally, I got released to go back to the barracks to use the latrine. We were standing in formation, waiting for everyone to form up, and my bladder just broke. I stood there in formation, standing at the perfect position of parade rest, eyes straight ahead. I never even flinched. Some might find it embarrassing, and at first it was, but as I stood with my drill sergeant yelling, my own urine running down my leg, I began to feel like a soldier. I was disgusted and embarrassed and, still, my military bearing was impeccable.

As soon as I was done, I was relieved to the barracks to take a shower and change my clothes. It was the first shower I got alone and, even better, it had lasted over three minutes. That, by itself, almost made the whole incident worth it.

When I returned outside, my drill sergeant asked me what had happened, and I explained it was because I didn't want to get anyone else smoked simply because I had to use the latrine. After that, they removed the rule. And he told me about when he himself had an accident flying in a chopper. Since then, I've heard many stories from others about being in the same type of situations, and having to pee in much odder places than myself. It turns out that it's just a part of the whole "adapt and overcome" thing they teach you.

The rest of basic training was pretty much text book. We had physical training, rifle ranges, road marches, the gas chamber, and tactical training exercises. At the very end I managed to catch pneumonia. The fire guard caught me wrapped up in a blanket, wearing sweats and my whole mop gear, shivering and hugging the toilet. She reported me to the drill sergeant, who then agreed to let me finish my final field training exercise physical fitness test before he brought me to the hospital. I was in the final week, but receiving quarters would have caused me to have to start the training all over again. I would have rathered to sufferone more week than redo the last eight.

After basic training was completed, I went to my Advanced Individual Training, or my AIT, at Fort Jackson, South Carolina. I was assigned to Delta Company 187 and trained as a 63S. All jobs in the military referred to a two digit number and a letter called an MOS. At the time a 63S was a heavy wheeled vehicle mechanic.

# That September Day

AIT, OR MOS TRAINING, VARIES in length. Mine was ten weeks long. However, because of my basic training date, I arrived at the school early; so I was there for a total of thirteen. I was there from the end of August until November. And I was there on September 11, 2003.

Still, to this day, I remember the exact moment I found out that a plane had hit the Twin Towers. We were sitting in the classroom waiting for the class to get started, and one of the instructors came in telling us that a plane had crashed into the towers. We didn't know how much damage was inflicted, and we all thought it was a fluke accident. The instructor would leave for a minute and check the news and then come back and give us an update.

We still didn't know what happened when we found out a tower hit the Pentagon. The only real worry was for a fellow soldier's father who was working there at the time. We couldn't see the news ourselves. We just knew that it wasn't an accident anymore. We didn't know how many planes were involved or what was hit.

We started to talk amongst ourselves, waiting for the class to start and, then, just a few minutes after we heard that the Pentagon was hit, our drill sergeant emerged in the door and hurried us out the building. We formed out and double-timed all the way back to our barracks.

We were immediately sent to our rooms, and had no idea why or what was going on. Some of the girls in our hall started breaking out the radios that they had stashed trying to see what was going on. Even so, often we'd take turns going up to the drill sergeant on duty to ask him a question so that we could peer over and get a look at the news on the TV.

I don't remember how long after that we were told what had actually happened. That day itself, and sitting in the barracks waiting and wondering, seemed like it went on forever. We had gone on total lock down and, while we were sitting there trying to figure out what this meant for us and what was going to happen next, I couldn't stop thinking about a comment that Tim had once made to me when he found out I joined the Army. We were sitting in the car and he asked me what would happen if we went to war. My comment was that, last time we went anywhere, I was in the second grade. He looked at me and said, "If you enlist, we're going to war." The way he looked at it was it was Murphy's Law; anything that can happen will. If I joined, then the worst would happen.

Everyone thought that we would be deploying right away. We spent the next two months of our training eagerly awaiting the word on what kind of action our country would take. By November, I was graduated and I got to go home for two weeks of leave, and then on to my active duty station in Fort Hood, Texas.

# On My Own

BASIC TRAINING AND AIT WAS the first time that I had really left home for anything more than a weekend trip to go visit somebody. Fort Hood was my first duty station and, like many other soldiers, it was the first time I was truly out on my own.

I lived in military barracks with one other roommate. We split the room down the side so as to each have our own space, but we shared a small little kitchen and a bathroom. I had been doing normal household things, like buying groceries and helping pay bills, when my previous boyfriend had his place. But it was different this time because it was my place. Granted, I was subject to barracks inspections and was forced to live with a roommate. But I also didn't have to pay rent or utilities, so it was a fair trade off.

Every day I reported to formation at 0600 hours for Physical Training, also called PT, and then I would go to work in the motor pool at 0900. We worked until around 1700 each day and then the rest of the day was usually mine. I would go hang out with friends, take dance classes and, twice a week, I would go to school at night. Sometimes, it almost felt like living in a dorm. Every weekend there was always a party or a bar to go to. You'd always have people that drank way too much to look after. Occasionally, one would pass out on the lawn. Normally, that guy was Hardman.

Hardman was a mechanic but worked as the unit armor when I got there. He was a typical old redneck, and I loved him to death. We became friends pretty quickly. Me, him, and another one of our friends, used to run around together all the time. I remember one time when we all went camping together in the winter. Don't know why we did it, but I do remember waking up and all of milk jugs being frozen, ripping my favorite of pants, and never catching a single fish.

Being in the Army and being stationed at Fort Hood was the first time I ever had one regular group of friends that I ran around with. I had plenty of friends in high school, but I was that girl who got along with everyone; I never really had my own clique. There were about a half dozen of us that hung out together most of the time I was stationed there. Others came and left while I was there, because of moving or getting out. Still, it seemed that, for the most part, "Maintenance" was always a very close-knit group, and I loved it.

We would have barbeques and go out to the bar together. I took turns dragging a few of them to ballet with me in Austin. One even spent an evening with me in the emergency room. When we were together, there was never a shortage of fun.

Thursday to Sunday always seemed like it was a nonstop party. We'd get off from Sergeant's time training at 1500 on Thursday and then it would begin. Friday morning we were usually all worn out, and you could smell the alcohol pouring off the maintenance platoon during the company runs.

We worked hard and we played hard. We broke a few rules here and there, but we never did anything that was in dereliction of our duty. We put our jobs first and, when we did do stupid things, it was on our own time; and we were lucky enough we never got caught. One time, we all had to run from the MPs because we got caught lighting fireworks off the roof. We tossed a rope over the side and all just went sliding down. My hands were blistered for weeks from the rope burn. Hardman was again the guilty party for that.

The only time we really ever had to deal with the law was on our trip to Mexico. Four of us had decided to take a Saturday excursion to the border. Two of us were sober; me, because I didn't really drink much, and the other because he was driving. The other two, however, were completely toasted. The worst thing about driving with drunken people isn't the loudness or stupidity, but rather that they have to stop to use the restroom every fifteen minutes.

At one point they started yelling that we needed to stop so they could pee. We were no more than five miles from the rest area and said they couldn't take it anymore, so we pulled over and let them out. It was mainly desert, so they went all the way down a good seventy-five yards to where a fence line and some brush was. Then, when they started coming back, we thought it would be funny to take off and make them have to run and try to jump in. Well, another car saw us and had reported it. Twenty minutes later, we were getting pulled over by police. They came from each direction and just swarmed the vehicle. There must have been about seven or eight cop cars there. They got out and surrounded us. We heard a tap on the window and expected to see a police officer with a night stick. Instead, we saw one with an M4.

We looked around, and the border patrol had surrounded our vehicle, all armed with M4s pointed straight at us. It turned out that the fence line was also the border between the U.S. and Mexico. Someone saw the two guys running for our car and they thought we were smuggling in illegal immigrants, so they called the border patrol. They checked our IDs and let us go, but the whole thing was definitely a different experience. I can't say I ever imagined being on the opposite side of one of our own rifles.

The friends I made at Fort Hood are ones that I'll never forget. I'll always have stories to tell and memories to look back on. One of the great things about the military is its comradery. Your fellow soldiers become your battle buddies, your friends, and your family. You see them and work with them every day. To be successful, you must trust them and rely on them, and, even when the mission is over, when you go home at the end of the day, you still always know they will be there tomorrow and you can count on them to watch your back.

Having good soldiers, ones who you can trust and rely on, is one of the key factors in having a successful team. The other is good Non-Commissioned Officers, or NCOs. The job of a good NCO is to make sure the mission is complete, as well as take care of the troops.

# Meeting John

WHEN I GOT TO FORT HOOD, I was assigned to the 53rd Quartermaster Company. At first, I was unhappy about it, because my drill sergeant told us the two places you don't want to go to are a postal unit or a petroleum unit (as far as being a mechanic), and I ended up in a petroleum unit. But it turned out for the best. I made a couple of really good friends, became good at my job, earned the rank of Corporal and, best of all, met my husband.

John was assigned to the $602^{nd}$ Maintenance Company, which was our company's third shop; basically, the guys who did the work we weren't allowed to. I was at his company almost every day. We lived across the courtyard from each other. I knew several guys from his unit and, yet, we never met. It wasn't until November 16th, a year after being stationed there, that our paths finally crossed.

One Saturday, I had gone to change the oil on my car, which was parked behind his barracks. Several people from his unit were having a barbeque. I had already had an invitation to the party, but left it as undecided. On my way out to the car, a few of the guys I knew yelled down from one of the balconies for me to join them. I waved at them and told them I was busy. However, curiosity got the best of me and, when I realized my filter was tight, I used it for an excuse to go up and borrow a filter wrench and check out the party.

One of the guys lent me one, making me promise that, after I was finished, I would come up and have a drink with them. I said okay and, when I was finished with my car, went back and hung out for the evening.

I only knew a hand full of people there, but talked to them and introduced myself to a few others, including the cute guy running the grill. We got to talking, and I would go back and forth between talking to him and my other friends there I knew. He was stationed behind the barbeque grill all evening so, every now and then, I would go back to get a small bite to eat as an excuse to talk to him.

After going back and forth a few times, our conversations began getting longer and longer. We talked about cars, our units, the Army and other little things. At one time, I remember talking about food, probably because he was grilling at the time, and one of his favorite dishes was biscuits and gravy. He said if he could find a girl that made good biscuits and gravy he'd marry her. He didn't know it at the time, but as it just so happens, biscuits and gravy is one of my best dishes.

I went to walk away once more and he asked me where I was going. I said, "Over there," or something to that effect. He looked at me and **said,** "You're not going anywhere. You're mine now." I must admit it was a cheesy line, but it did the **trick.** I turned right around and sat back down. I **didn't** know it at the time, but he was normally a **really** shy guy. None of his friends could believe he was talking to me.

At the end of the night, the person who was originally supposed to be my date offered to walk me home. John found out and insisted that he would do it instead. We had to go around the long way because I was underage and had been drinking, and my motor sergeant was walking around on duty. He was one of those types who was always looking to bust people. And there would be no mercy if I were caught. We went in the back way, and dashed in my door when we thought he wasn't looking. Apparently he saw us, but had thought we went into another room.

He came up the stairs to knock on their door and, just about then, the fire alarm went off. John must have thought I was nuts because I told him to get in the bathroom and refused to let him leave, paranoid at what would happen if we got caught.

We were in the bathroom for what must have been over an hour waiting for the fire department to clear the building. We sat and talked some more, and, when the fire alarm went silent, he went and sat down on my bed (I didn't have a chair in my room). I went back into the bathroom to use the facilities. By the time I came back out, he was passed out on my bed. I tried to wake him, but he wouldn't budge. So I put a blanket over him let him sleep.

When he woke up the next morning, he apologized and went to his room saying that he'd give me a call. I can't say that I really expected to hear from him. I assumed he would just think that I was some crazy chick that locked him in her room. But sure enough, later the same evening, he gave me a call and asked if I wanted to go get something to eat.

After that time we were inseparable. We went everywhere and did everything together. When I got off work he'd be standing at the balcony waiting for me. He'd call my phone when he saw me walk up the stairs. Less than two weeks later, he was skipping his family dinner to have Thanksgiving dinner with me. Come Christmas, I had skipped out on my own family plans to be with him.

# I Do

JOHN AND I MET IN THE middle of November. We were only together about five weeks before I went home with him for Christmas. We arrived at his mom's house the day before Christmas. Since John had been in Beaumont, TX, loading trucks, he hadn't done his shopping yet, so he left me there and took off with his brother. He left me with his mother and his brother's girlfriend, who I had only known for about fifteen minutes. I felt kind of weird at first; being left with people I didn't know.

When I heard his car pull up I went running outside to meet him. I opened up the door and saw him with a large teddy bear in his hands. Worried that I ruined the surprise, I went back inside hoping that he didn't see me.

That night we stayed up talking and, at about 3 a.m., I had to get up and use the bathroom. I walked through the living room and saw the teddy bear under the tree. At this point, I was already well aware of what I was getting for Christmas, or so I thought.

When I returned from the bathroom, I noticed that he was hiding something in his hand. I asked him what he was doing, and he just kind of looked at me for a minute. Then he said it was Christmas and asked me if I wanted my present.

Of course, I said, "Yes," and thought he was going to let me go get my teddy bear out from under the tree. Then he opened up his hand. And in it was a small jewelry box. He opened it up, looked up at me, and asked me if I would marry him. I was speechless. I threw my arms around him and just squeezed him as hard as I could. I was in total disbelief. I don't remember at what point I was actually able to answer him.

The next morning we told his family. His mother, brother, and soon-to-be sister-in-law were very happy and congratulated us. After opening presents, we went to his father's house where it turned out I had many more soon-to-be in-laws to meet. His family all smiled about us and treated me politely. I got to watch them all sit around and play music together and I began to think that this was a family that I would really come to like and fit in with.

Because of the time difference, we had told all of John's family before we had told mine. When I called them, it was a totally different reaction. My mother congratulated me but seemed a little concerned because we hadn't been together long. And my dad ended up leaving my grandmother's house and refused to talk to anyone. It took the whole day and my brother chasing him down to get him to calm down and accept it.

We really hadn't been together long, so I understand where they were coming from. I was caught a little off guard myself and, when people kept asking when we were getting married, I didn't know what to say. We started talking about maybe in the summer or in the fall. But, like the rest of our relationship, that, too, came much faster.

After the Christmas break we found out that both of our companies were possibly getting deployed, so we began to look at closer dates. And the more real the chance became we were getting deployed, the closer that date became. We didn't want to risk planning a big wedding just to have it ruined because one of us was gone. So, when we finally picked a date, it was the end of January. And the date we picked was February 8th, only two weeks away.

I called my family and told them we were coming home in two weeks for a few days and that they would finally get to meet John. This was a good thing because they had not yet met this man whom I was planning to marry. Then I told them we were going to get married while I was there. I think it may have been a surprise at first, but everybody jumped up and started to pitch in to get everything together.

You may think two weeks is quick notice, but I highly recommend it. There was no stress involved.

No worrying about how the flower arrangements that I picked out eight months ago weren't right, or the colors on the table didn't match the colors of the dresses, and how all the planning that was done went to hell. Instead, the only thing we cared about was that we were there with each other.

We got married at sunset in a bar with floor-to-ceiling windows, overlooking the ocean. John wore his dress uniform and I wore a rum and ivory dress. A harpist played as I walked down the aisle, and my entire family was there. It was utterly beautiful. The only other thing that we could have asked for was that his family was there.

The only one from John's side of the family who made it was his mother. His brother wanted to go but his fiancé was pregnant and wasn't able to fly, and he wouldn't leave her. The rest of his family didn't even try.

When we told them about it, they said they couldn't come because they couldn't afford the tickets. When we offered to pay, they said it was because they couldn't miss work. To this day, they still hold to that story. They say it was too short of notice. But, only a few days before we actually got married, his stepmother had called me while I was in the dressing room at the bridal store and tried to talk me out of marrying him. She went so far as to say that she couldn't believe he was going to marry someone like me. Right then I knew my warm welcome into the family was not what it appeared.

I didn't tell John about the incident for some time after. I kept it to myself. And, a few days later, we were happily married, ready to spend the rest of our lives together... kind of.

# The First Time

FOR A GOOD PORTION OF the time John and I were dating, he was assigned to load up trucks for deployment in Beaumont, Texas. In fact, in the less than three months we were together before we got married, he was gone for nearly two of them. We didn't much like the time apart, but he was only assigned down there for December and January. And every weekend I would drive down to visit him. We made the best out of it, but we didn't know that it was about to get much worse. Beaumont was only a preview of what our lives were going to be like.

The week after John and I got back from getting married; both of our companies had deployment orders for Iraq. At first, I wasn't bothered by it. I remember, when I got the orders, I was so excited to finally be getting deployed. Ever since September 11th, I had been prepared to deploy. Another unit in my battalion was deployed in 2002 as a part of Operation Enduring Freedom. I volunteered to go with them, but I didn't hold the right MOS.

I was sad about having to leave John after

being newly married. But much of the excitement of the deployment helped in that, since we would both be over there at the same time, it was only going to be six months apart. So even if we weren't to deploy anywhere near each other, six months would be something we could handle.

Our company began to prepare. We loaded up our CONEX (military shipping containers), shipped out our vehicles, went thought medical processing, and, the whole time, I remained excited and eager to go. Then came the day we were to be issued out Desert Camouflage Uniform, or DCUs. It was about a week before we were supposed to leave. And I found out I was pregnant. I wasn't going. I had waited so long to get deployed and now I wasn't going

I tried to get a waiver to deploy. I begged and pleaded, thinking there was some loophole. I had heard about people going overseas pregnant; they just had to be back by seven months. But this was a combat zone and, no matter how much I wished for it, it wasn't happening. So I eventually sucked it up and tried to deal with the fact I wasn't going.....but my husband was. I think that was probably the worst part for me, too. I was dying to go, and he really didn't care to. Yet he was getting to go and I was stuck staying back.

Then the realizations got worse. Not only was I not getting to deploy but, because John was, I was now going to have to be home all alone with my husband and all my friends overseas. I was already scared about being pregnant. And now I was going to be pregnant alone.

I was sad and a little bit worried but I just kept telling myself, "I can do six months. I can do six months." I was only two months pregnant when he left and we figured that he would be back when I was eight months along; just in time to be there for the birth of our first child. Of course, we didn't want to be apart but, as long as he was back before I gave birth, we were okay with it. No one ever thought that it was going to last this long. Nor did I ever imagine that it would be that hard.

When I saw John off, I didn't want to be like all the other wives who sat there and cried and made it hard. So I brought him to his company, I gave him a hug and a kiss, told him I loved him and I would see him in a few months, and then left. I barely got out of the parking lot when I started crying. I think, deep down, I really knew that it wasn't just going to be a few months.

I'm not one to cry because I miss somebody. Heck, I'm not even usually one to miss somebody at all. When all the girls in basic were upset because they missed their family or their boyfriends, I was looking forward to my new adventure. They had pictures of their loved ones in their wall lockers. Me, I had pictures of my car.

But this time it was different; maybe because I

didn't know exactly where he was going, when he would return, or if he would be safe. Maybe it was because we were just married. Or maybe it was because I was pregnant and full of hormones. But I cried, more than I ever cried in my life. I had to pull the car over on the way home because I couldn't see the road through my tears. It wasn't just that night, either. It was the next night, and the night after that.

*17 April 02*
*Dear John,*

*I already miss you so much. I feel like I'm going to bust. I came home today, saw the pics Sandy sent, then cried. Next I sat on the couch, found the red squishy yo-yo thing, Then cried.*

*Then after several hours of feeling sad I got enough in me to get up and get something to eat, so I put on your slippers, and then I cried. I guess I'm just a big cry baby, but I miss you so much. I just need you so bad it hurts. At least it's one day down and one day closer to you coming home.*

*I'll keep it short since I really don't have an address and I'll end up sending you these all once I get it. That and you probably don't want to read a bunch of babble.*

*Just know that I'm thinking about you and I love you a lot.*

*Hugs & Kisses,*
*Love,*
*Jenna Jaye*

# Trying To Stay In Touch

IT WAS ALMOST THREE MONTHS before I started getting letters from John. Other people I knew were already getting letters from their spouses, and I was starting to get so worried because I hadn't yet gotten one. I didn't think anything had happened to him. I had been in the military long enough to know that no news is good news, but I was worried that maybe he had a change of heart. By the time he had been deployed for three months, we had spent more time apart than together.

I opened my mailbox every day praying for a letter. Then, one day, I finally got my first one. My mailbox was flooded with letters. I must have had over a dozen letters waiting for me, and I sat down and read them all at once. The post marks started just a few days after he left, but the mail system was so bad at the time that everything was delayed.

John received much of his letters the same way. I didn't have an address for him, but I wanted to talk to him so badly that I would write him a letter everyday and then set it aside until I heard from him. I began to number them so that he could read them in order when he received them. The first set of numbers goes up to fifteen, and then I just started to write the dates on the envelope seal.

Communication was the hardest thing about his deployment. It was hard enough just trying to get to know one another through letters, but trying to pass news about events and his family was even worse.

*03 July 03*
*Dear John,*
*I had a dream about us last night. We were sitting on the front porch, Georgia was in my lap and you were sitting next to us playing guitar. It was a warm summer evening, and we were just sitting there together, rocking back and forth as we listened to you play music.*
*I miss you so much, love. I was talking to your mom and she said that Popi is sick again and they don't think he's going to make it much longer. I'm sorry to tell you this in a letter, because I try to write them to cheer you up and I know that this does the exact opposite to you.*
*Unfortunately, I don't think you can have emergency leave until he passes away………I know he means a lot to you. Hopefully he'll be okay until you come home. It's cancer, so you never know how much time you'll get. My grandmother lived for almost 17 years after the day they told her she only had 2 years left.*
*Just pray. It's about all we can do now.*
*Love Always,*
*Jenna Jaye*

John had a good enough command that they let him come home about a month later when Popi's condition worsened. He was able to be there when he passed away. Thanks to the Red Cross, emergency information was one thing that soldiers were able to get in a timely manner. Messages regarding deaths, births and major hospitalizations are able to reach soldiers in almost any situation and location.

About a month or so after his leave ended and he returned to country, communication managed to improve significantly. Mail still often took a month to arrive. But John and the soldiers in the unit began to get access to internet and phones more regularly. I received phone calls about two or three times a month and an e-mail about once a week. Near the end we were even able to use the Army's instant messenger program.

# Georgia

ONLY NINE MONTHS AND FIVE days after my husband and I were married, we had our daughter.

Originally, when we got married, we had planned to wait to have children. Well, at least I wanted to wait. John's brother was getting ready to have a baby and, when John would bring the subject up to me, I would say five years. He joked about maybe five months. And then, five weeks later, I was pregnant.

I didn't find out right away. I was in the middle of my deployment process and just went through SRP, Solider Readiness Processing, where they administer your shots and give you a pregnancy test. Somehow they missed it and I, along with one of my battle buddies, came up negative. We were both given the anthrax and smallpox vaccinations, among other things.

I only found out because my butt had started to get really big and John was cracking jokes about me being pregnant. So I took a pregnancy test to prove him wrong and, instead, I ended up proving him right.

I had thought about hiding the pregnancy, and trying to deploy for as long as I could until they sent me back. But I worried about the shots I was given. So I went and got checked out to make sure everything was okay. Unfortunately, by doing so, I was outing myself in the process. I knew that going to the doctor would get my pregnancy put on record and prevent me from being able to deploy. But one of my NCOs who knew told me she had two miscarriages trying to hide her own pregnancies. I wasn't willing to take that chance.

After everyone found out, and I knew I was non-deployable, I began to beg for my command to allow me to go with them, to see if there was a waiver I could sign, or be allowed to go until "so far" into my term. But I could not. I'm sure I wouldn't have enjoyed being deployed pregnant. But there are women who try to get out of deployment by getting pregnant and I didn't want to be labeled as one of them. On top of that, I had waited so long to deploy. And, now that I was finally going to get to deploy, I was going to miss my chance. To make it worse, John was still going with his unit. So now my husband and all of my friends had left for another country and left me behind.

I managed to adapt and made friends with a few other females that were back with me, because they were pregnant too. In fact, our battalion was left with so many pregnant women that they began a pregnancy PT program in the morning. I stayed in pretty good shape and was even doing pushups well into my 7th month.

When it came time to have my daughter, I had decided to go home since my husband and almost all of my friends were deployed. Being a first-time mom, I wanted to deliver and spend my convalescent leave at home where I would have family to help. Getting home proved more difficult than I thought. It almost took an act of congress to get my leave approved… literally.

*06 Oct 06*
*Dear John,*
*I'm typing this letter because I'm too pissed and upset to write. I have a million things running through my head at once and I'm going lose it.*

*I keep getting told that I need to have this, or I need to have this to go on leave. I have my pregnancy profile, a letter from my doctor, my medical records, and copies of all the Army regs. I got it through the company finally but now the CSM says he won't sign it. It's complete bs. I'm having a hard enough time not having you around for this. I need to be with my family.*

*I want the waiting room to be full of happy anxious family members who all go outside and light up a cigar after she's born. I want to be visited by people who actually care about her and are excited as can be just to look through the nursery window and see her. Not some Army wives and CSM that could care less about me or her and only there to be polite and save face.*

*More than just that, I'm doing terrible here. You leaving the second time was a lot harder than the first. I just can't take it. Even though I know you love me and you're coming back, my heart still feels broken. It's like you left me and I'll never see you again. I can't make it a day without getting depressed about you being gone. I break down and cry for no reason...... ...*

*I'm gonna crash now. All this being upset and worrying has made me tired. I can't wait until you come home and bring me to my senses, I really do need you. I hope you know that. Without you I feel like life is going haywire and there's nothing I can do to fix it. But when I'm with you, it doesn't matter what's wrong. I guess that's because as long as I have you everything else is just a minor detail.*

*I miss you so much,*
*Your loving wife,*
*Jenna Jaye*

When I had first put my leave in to go home, it was turned down. I would have had the leave, regardless, because I was having a child and the leave I wanted to take prior was my normal accrued leave. But my battalion commander turned down the leave because he said there was no reason for me to go home.

One of the individuals in my company had remarked that I should call my congressman. Instead, I called my mom. I was upset and was trying to explain to her what had happened. She asked if there was anything I could do about it. I didn't think there was but, instead of saying no, I made a sarcastic comment along the lines of, "Yeah, call my congressmen." Apparently, she wanted me home as bad as I wanted to be home. When I got off the phone, she had called my grandpa who called whoever else and, by the next morning, when I walked into the office there was a "congressional" sitting on my battalion commander's desk. Needless to say, I got my leave. Unfortunately, the saga didn't end there.

I went home at the end of October; a few weeks prior to when I was due. After only being home a week, my unit called every other day to see if I had delivered yet. On the 8$^{th}$ of November, I was sick of being pregnant. Already forty weeks, I decided to go old-fashion and drink castor oil, having read that it was used to help cause contractions. It worked, kind of. It started my contractions within a few hours. I took it Friday night and, on Saturday morning, I was admitted into the hospital. My contractions were two minutes apart but I was not dilating. They kept me there for a while but, eventually, sent me home since I was not progressing. The castor oil had done its job of inducing contractions, but it did not induce labor.

When I went into the hospital, I had called my unit to let them know I was admitted to the hospital, as is protocol. When I was released, I called them back to change my status. The next day the battalion commander was ordering that I return. My rear detachment commander got them to extend my leave by a few more days but was told, if I didn't deliver by then, I was to come home. There would not be another extension. And he didn't care if I had my baby on the plane.

On the 12th, I was overdue enough that the doctor had made arrangements to induce my labor. I was supposed to arrive at the hospital that morning but, the night before, my contractions began to get even worse. I had been having them ever since that Saturday. And now they were at the point to where I almost couldn't bear it.

My mother took me to the hospital at about 5 a.m. and, at 7 a.m., my water broke. My family all came to the hospital when they heard the news and stood by anxiously in the waiting room. Several hours went by and nothing; a few more hours and still nothing.

By 11 p.m., I was only dilated five centimeters. I was trying to have natural child birth, with no drugs, but, at this point, they told me that giving me an epidural would help me progress as well as help me get some much needed sleep, so I took it.

Within twenty minutes, I was fast asleep and I didn't wake back up till about 1:30 in the morning when I was fully dilated. The midwife on duty came in and I began to push. But the baby was what they called "sunny side up" and wouldn't come out. It took the suction cup and three hours of pushing until, at 4:52 a.m., she was finally born.

John kept calling every few hours to check up on me. I remember talking to him on the phone during labor and him telling me "Hold on"; then pulling the phone away as I pushed; then getting back on and talking to him again. I tried to keep a calm normal voice when I was on the phone. But, at one point, he asked me what I was doing and I remember yelling, "I'm having a kid! What the hell do you think I'm doing?"

I think that was about the only time I really snapped during the labor. But I like the fact that, when I did it, it was at him. John had been deployed almost my entire pregnancy, so he never was able to experience any of it. Getting to yell at him that once was kind of my "You did this to me" moment.

After Georgia was born, I sent John plenty of pictures, and even some video of her, but I know it wasn't the same. He never got to hold her that day in the hospital when she was first born; never saw her first smile or heard her first laugh. Like a lot of other soldiers serving in Iraq, he now had a child he had never seen before and had only heard about from others.

# Love At First Sight

WHEN JOHN FINALLY CAME HOME from Iraq, Georgia was five and a half months old. It was the first time she had ever got to see her father and the first time her father was able to hold her in his arms.

When he arrived, his company was taken to one of the gyms on post where the families would be able to greet them and finally get to take them home. I remember spending all day with one of his friends' wives getting ready. I had done my hair and picked out a plain old ivory dress that I had in my closet to wear. It was simple, and I knew he had seen it before, but I chose it so that I could show off my new figure which I had gained from having a child.

I put Georgia in a new pretty pink dress that I had gotten for just the occasion, along with white and pink lace headband and matching socks. I also stocked the fridge up with things he liked and made his favorite strawberry cake with cream cheese frosting. Best of all, though, I thought, would be the new car that I had bought him. It was his dream car. And it was waiting in the parking lot with a yellow ribbon and his name written really big on a tag covering the front windshield.

All the families were piled in the gym awaiting their loved ones. And as they began to file in and get in formation in front us, people were picking out their spouses and their sons. I recognized a few people here and there but, at first, I could not pick out John. As their commander gave his speech, I failed to hear anything because I was looking so intently for the husband I barely knew. Just then, before they were released, I saw him standing in the back row. Suddenly, I felt lost. I didn't know what I was going to do or what I was going to say. When the commander finally released them, I just stood there against the wall as the rest of the families began to crowd the gymnasium floor.

I watched John as he looked around for me, and he looked just as puzzled. When he finally spotted me, I think it took him a minute to be sure that it was indeed me. He walked over to me and I just continued to stand there, trying ever so hard not to cry. I gave him a quick hug and then handed him Georgia. After that, I was out of the picture.

From the moment he held her, they were inseparable. Nothing else seemed to matter. Not me. Not his new car. Nothing. When we got home, he just sat on the couch holding her in disbelief; as though he just now found out he had a daughter for the first time. That night we all slept in bed together; John on the left, me on the right, and Georgia in the middle.

The next day, we did the same thing. This time, as we all laid there and he sat playing with her and smiling, then, not even forty-eight hours after being home, she looked up at him and said "dada." It was her first word and he was there for it. To this day, I still believe that was his proudest moment and is still his most cherished memory. It is four years later, and he still talks about it regularly.

Ever since he and Georgia met for the first time, there has been a bond. It was as though she automatically knew that this was her father. Even now she's been a complete daddy's girl. I can put her to sleep in her bed but, no matter what, when I wake up, I almost always find her in our bed or on the couch, wherever it is that daddy is sleeping. If she gets up in the middle of the night and he's on the computer, she'll lie down and sleep on the living room floor.

# A Broken Heart

SOON AFTER JOHN GOT BACK from Iraq, we both came up on our end of time in service, or ETS, meaning our contracts were up and we were now able to get out. I, myself, had wanted to stay in and reenlist, but John did not. And, since we knew that staying in could mean one deployment after another and not being able to have a normal family life, we agreed to both get out.

John and I had not been married for long before he left so, when he returned, it was almost as though we had to start all over again. We had our differences when it came to taking care of Georgia; where we would live and what we would do for work. The biggest problem we had, though, was that it seemed like we didn't know each other. We had written back and forth while he was gone, but it just wasn't the same as having a relationship together in person. In certain ways, we grew closer over the duration of his deployment but, in other ways, we grew further apart.

When we got out of the Army, we moved out of Texas and back to John's home town in Georgia. We stayed with his family in a house they would soon be moving out of and which we could then rent from them. It seemed like a good idea, because the rent would be cheaper and we could get established. But it was hard for me for John to have his family and for me to have no one. I missed my job, I missed the Army, and I missed having friends and people to talk to. I was worried that things were not going to work between me and John, and then the inevitable came.

We were lying in bed one morning, talking about life; what we're going to do as far as work, hopes for the future, and about our relationship. I started to tell him how I had been feeling and I made the mistake of asking him if he still loved me. I expected a sweet "Yes, baby" or "Of course, I do," but instead he looked at me and said, "I love you … I'm just not in love with you anymore."

My heart was crushed. I didn't know what I was going to do. I knew that I had already said I would stay with him no matter what. And that I didn't want to get a divorce. As much as it bothered me, I couldn't say I blamed him. When he left, we had only been together for a short while and had barely lived together. I'm sure he felt as though he was just like someone's boyfriend when he left but, now that he had returned, he was a husband and a father. It must have been a change for him. He went from being all alone in Iraq to coming home to a family overnight. I often referred to his situation as *instant family*, meaning he woke up and, all of a sudden, he instantly had a family.

As much as it hurt me, we woke up the next day and acted almost as though it had never happened. I loved him more than anything, and I was willing to endure whatever I had to do to try and get him back. I couldn't imagine what it must have been like for him. So I stayed, hoping to myself that he would find, once again, the love he had before.

# My Turn

I DELAYED MY IDEA OF going back to school, and started to look for a job. I did have an associate's degree which I had earned on active duty. But it didn't seem to do me any good. Every classified ad and job posting I could find said either high school diploma or bachelors degree; there was no in between. I was beginning to get extremely discouraged. And then I saw an ad for mechanics; prior service; preferably 63 series. I was excited and applied for it, hoping for the best. I did not realize at the time that the job was in Iraq.

The next day, my husband received a call back, for we had both applied for the job figuring we had better odds that one of us would get it. When the female voice told my husband the job was overseas, he immediately handed the phone to me. He told her that there's no way he was going, but try talking to my wife; she might want to.

The woman asked me about my background, told me about the position, and offered me the job. I was ecstatic. I finally had the opportunity to go to Iraq and I couldn't turn it down. We got out of active duty so that we wouldn't both spend our daughter's childhood deployed. But I couldn't get over the fact that I didn't go. So I went to work for a company called LSI, as a civilian contract mechanic.

I was excited to go for so many reasons. I was finally getting to serve my time. I knew that I would have a good job and not have to worry about bills but, also partly, because it would give me a chance to get away and think. John and I were doing much better. But I needed some time to myself and to think about everything.

While I was gone, I decided to start a new tradition. I had always written John while he was deployed, but I decided to start writing Georgia as well.

*30 Aug 04*
*Dear Georgia,*
*Hello my pumpkin pie. How are you? I know you are too little to read this, but hopefully daddy will read it to you. I am in a place called Dubai in the United Arab Emirates. Yesterday I was in Paris, France and tomorrow I will be in Baghdad, Iraq.*
*I know you don't know where these places are, but when you get older I will show you on a map so you can see all the places mommy has been.*
*Since last year when your father went to Iraq, we started to write each other letters and now we keep them all in a box. While I am gone I will write you a letter every week. Have daddy get you a box and you can start keeping them, too. Then one day*

*when you're older you can read back on them.*

*I miss you very much and I hope you know that.*
*I'll only be gone a few months and then I'll be home*
*for your birthday or Christmas. That's only about*
*17 weeks away. You and your daddy are my entire*
*world. I will be counting the days until I come*
*home.*

*Love,*
*Mommy*
*P.S. I enclosed a coin from this country for*
*something for you to keep. Have dad put it in a safe*
*place, so you don't lose it, or eat it. :)*

My first day in Iraq, I got to receive a taste of
what I had been missing. We were unloading the
plane, getting on busses to go into the main part of
base, and the sirens went off. They took us over to
an airport hangar at the end of the flight line that
was designated as a bunker. I remember sitting
there thinking *Welcome to Iraq.*

After we got an all clear and we boarded the
bus, one of the guys began to tell me how common
mortar rounds were there, in Anaconda. In the next
week, I was there waiting to get in-processed and
sent to the base where I would be working. Anaconda seemed to get a lot of mortar rounds, but it
was also a pretty nice and well established base so
it seemed to make up for it. I think I received more
mortar rounds on that base then I did the entire rest
of my deployment in Iraq, but I also got to order
pizza and go to the pool.

*06 Sept 04*
*Dear John,*

*I know your probably getting all my letters at the same time right now, but it's hard to find a place to drop it being I'm always in transit.*

*This place is definitely not what I expected. Anaconda was nice. Everyone had individual rooms, with a shared bathroom between each two. It had a movie theater, large gym, and indoor and outdoor pool. Last night I went to the pool and it was nice. It was Saddam's Olympic training pool. Also confined within the camp walls was the soccer field, where I was told his son had murdered all those Olympic athletes.*

*I guess I expected it to be more like in the field. Like in a tent, get crappy food, and rarely shower. Instead I'm eating Burger King, three-egg omelets, and taking long hot showers indoors. The weather is not nearly as hot either. I know that's because it's September and it's hotter in the summer months. But right now it's no hotter than July in Texas and I'm told it will only get better.*

*We'll I'm going to crash out. It's only 1 a.m. and I'm up because we got shelled. It was the closest one we've had so far it actually shook the trailer. I know that's not rare, but it was still the first one that I had that shook.*

*I love you and I miss you. I hope school is going okay. Take care and kiss my pumpkin pie.*
*Love,*
*Jenna Jaye*

For most the time I was there I worked in a small FOB (forward operating base) just south of Tikrit, called Remagen. There, I worked servicing and repairing trucks that drove through on convoy, and helped establish a motor pool from the ground up.

We worked out of maintenance tents and outside on a piece of concrete slab that the Local Nationals had poured for us. The closest thing we had to an office was a CONEX that we had covered with sand bags so that it would double as shelter during mortar attacks.

In the back, it had a small office with an A/C unit in it that we could use to cool down in the summer and a small floor heater we used to warm up with in the winter.

The motor pool had only the basics and was by far not the best around but, having been there from when they first raised the tents and set up, it felt like it was ours and was plenty sufficient for us to get the job done.

Our primary work consisted of inspecting and repairing trucks that came through on convoy. When different units passed through and stopped over at our base, they would leave their vehicles in a holding line and then go to chow and do whatever else they needed to do while we repaired their vehicles.

Trucks were often *deadlined* for repairs on parts that we could not replace. We would always do what we could to get parts from other vehicles that were down on post, or rig something up to try and make a temporary repair hold. But that wasn't always an option. There were many times where we let a truck go, knowing perfectly well that it was not mission capable. Once, when we had a convoy going through on its way to Sammar, it had two ambulances that were both deadlined. One was for various reasons and the other for a fuel leak.

In the true military spirit of "adapt and overcome," the vehicles rolled on anyway. That particular night we sat on top of the watch tower and watched as that unit lit up the sky in Samara which was only thirty clicks down the road.

It was almost like a bunch of teenagers sitting out in the summer watching fireworks. We were all piled into one little watch tower "ooh-ing" and "aah-ing" as all of the trucks rolled into the town and the bombs started to go off. It was too far away to hear anything but, just by the amount of glowing in the sky, you could imagine what was taking place.

Over the next few days, as the convoys came back through on their way north, I looked for the ambulance we had sent downrange with the fuel leak. Having an overactive imagination, I had thought the worst possible. That a flame or a spark from all the fire got near the truck and it and the passengers were all gone. Luckily, that wasn't so. They came back a few days later, fully intact, and with no problems on the truck.

The rest of the time, when we didn't have convoys coming through, we spent our time improving our area. Some of it was work related, some of it not. We eventually turned our outside slab into a basketball court and borrowed a mini backhoe from KBR to dig out a horseshoe pit. It definitely helped our long days go by a little bit quicker.

# Regret

MY FIRST LEAVE WAS SET for November. I was going to get to go home for Georgia's first birthday. I was so excited. I was really worried about having to miss things while I was over there and having trouble being gone from Georgia. But now I was going to get to go home for her birthday; her first birthday.

*18 Oct 04*
*Dear Georgia,*

*How is my beautiful girl? I miss you so much I can hardly wait to see you. I should be home on the 11th, two days before your birthday. I'm going to make you a chocolate cake with white frosting like I had on my first birthday. My personal favorite is devil's food with cream cheese frosting.*
*Would you like that? Or I could get you a strawberry, that's daddy's favorite. I got an idea. We'll go to the store and pick out that stuff together to make you cake.*

*I love you and I miss you,*
*Mommy*

I never got to go. My flight was canceled and I missed my beautiful little girl's first birthday.

*11 Nov 04*
*Dear Georgia,*

*Hey my beautiful baby girl. I'm sorry I haven't written you in a few weeks, but I thought that by now I would be home.*

*I tried very hard to make it back for your birthday, but all airspace has been closed to civilians. I missed my flight and have no chance getting a new one to make it by Saturday.*

*I miss you so much and it's so hard to be here when I think about how much you're growing. I saw your Halloween pictures and I can't believe daddy got your hair up into a pony tail. I hope that you have a good birthday on Saturday. I hear you're getting a Winnie the Pooh cake, and I'm sure you'll get lots of cool stuff. Daddy told me he was going to get you something to climb on. It's only going to be a couple of weeks until I get to come and play with you.*

*I can't wait till I can come home and play with you. I checked again today and as far as anyone can tell me they're still closed. I want to say I'll beat this letter home, but as in life there is nothing for sure except death and taxes.*

*I love you and miss you,*
*Take care of daddy for me,*
*Jenna Jaye*

The tour itself was supposed to be one year, but I only did a little over four months of it, from August to December. After my plans to go home for Georgia's birthday failed, it was my breaking point. I missed my daughter's first birthday and I couldn't forgive myself.

Things like that are common for the military. They miss all kinds of key events in the life of their family because of deployments. John, himself, had already missed the birth of his first child. But I was a civilian now which, to me, meant I missed it by choice. I was still proud that I had come to Iraq, but it didn't seem the same as if I had gone with my unit. I felt more like I was there for a paycheck then I was out of duty. And the last thing I wanted was my daughter to grow up and think that her mother had missed some of the most important moments in her life for a paycheck.

So the next chance I got, I took a flight home to go on leave and, as soon as I got home, I turned in my two weeks notice and never came back.

It's not that I had lost my desire to serve my country, but I didn't want my daughter to grow up thinking that I missed out on her life for a paycheck. If I was going back again, it would be with the Army and as a soldier.

# A Not So Normal Life

WHEN I CAME BACK FROM Iraq, I took the Holidays off and then, in January, began to look for a "normal job," the goal being to stay at home like a normal mom and a normal wife. As it turns out, I don't do normal so well. I put in resumes for every mechanic's job I could find, but I got nothing as a response. Not even a call back or an interview.

I began to wonder if it was because I was a female. So I began to submit two resumes for every job I applied; one for me and one for my husband. I wrote both resumes. And both were about the same except that, in mine, I had added that I had been a Non-commissioned Officer and had an associate's degree. I used my maiden name and put two separate addresses and phone numbers on them.

Soon after, John began to get responses, but I still got nothing. The only response I ever did get from all of my applications and efforts, was a seven-dollar-per-hour, entry-level, no-experience-required job. Eventually, I found a job with an independent shop that had only a few other employees. It then got sold only two weeks after I took the position. Then, the new owner offered to keep me on, dropping my seventeen percent commission salary to seven dollars an hour. I was the youngest one there by at least ten years, and the only female, and the only one he made this offer to. Needless to say, I told him where to go. The down side ended up being that this shop was now the only reference I had.

When I got hired, the owner knew I was interviewing for another job. It was not a job that I had applied for; rather one that had found me through a military hiring website. They called me, told me about the job, and asked if I would be interested in a phone interview. I said yes. And soon after my phone interview, I had been flown out for a second, and then a third interview. Most of the other people applying for jobs at the same time as me were much older, much more educated, and much more experienced than me. The entire time, I couldn't believe they were looking at me for the job.

The company was Eaton. They make something like eighty-five percent of the transmissions on the market for large commercial trucks. I was very excited about it and thought it would be a position that I really liked, so I continued on with the interview process.

After the third interview, one of the gentlemen drove me back to the airport and told me that I had impressed everyone, and that I was the only one that they were looking at for the position. He said they just had to finish my background check and then should be calling me in a few days with a salary offer. Then I never heard from them again.

At the time, I had not had a lot of experience in applying for civilian jobs, let alone a job for a large corporation, so I was unaware that it was expected of me to check up on the position after a certain time. I still, to this day, don't know what happened. But the only thing I can imagine is that when they called my current place of employment, the new owner, who I recently gave my opinion of to, was the one who answered the phone.

# Living Life Four Months at a Time

I HAD PRETTY MUCH GIVEN up. I was not working, so I had no income, and I felt like I was never going to get a job. Then I saw a listing for a National Guard recruiting job and I went for it. Within a week of seeing the recruiter, I was sworn in and had a full time position. Once again, the military had saved me.

Ever since I got out of the Army, I had been bouncing around. I was out of the Army a little less than four months before I went to work in Iraq. I only spent a little over four months there before I came back home. And then I had gone for four months unemployed, not knowing what I was going to do.

Now that I had my recruiting job, I figured I was set. I was back in the military and living at home while I did it. In April, I went to Arkansas for recruiting school. I was gone for five weeks and, shortly after that, I was back home and ready to dive into my new job. I hadn't always liked recruiters but, because I love the military and truly think that it is a great way for people get ahead in life, I figured it would be the perfect job for me. John got a job at a local trucking company, and we began to settle down and look for a house.

Recruiting, however, wasn't turning out to be what I hoped. I still really liked the idea of doing it, but it was summer and really slow. I always "made my numbers," or rather enlisted my required amount, but I spent most of my time bored in my office or outside smoking to kill time. There were no schools to attend or events to go to, and cold-calling off a list was not my thing. I believe being a recruiter should not just be about putting in the best people, but also helping someone find what's best for them. Otherwise put, I wouldn't put in anyone that I wasn't willing to go to war with. And I wouldn't put someone in if I thought they had better options. More than once, I sent a person to the active Army recruiter, or even a recruiter for another branch of service.

It was now August, and I knew school would be starting soon, and then recruiting would start to be more interesting because I would get to start going to places and talking to people about the Guard and the military. I would get to offer people a way to go to school and change their lives; to do all the things that I had wanted to be a recruiter for. Then, out of nowhere, John got fired.

I had asked him to look around for another job because his hours were terrible and, after spending so much of our marriage apart, I wanted to start spending it together. When his employer found out that he had been looking for another position, they told him they were sorry he wasn't happy there and then fired him. Now he wasn't working, and there was no way we were going to get a house. We talked about him finding another job, or possibly going back to school.

WyoTech was the school we had always wanted to attend while we were in the Army. I had actually wanted to go there prior to joining the Army but could not afford it. Part of my original reason for joining was so that I could afford to pay for it when I got out.

We eventually decided on him going to WyoTech. We figured that, since we didn't yet own a home, only had one child, and now no job, it was the perfect chance for him to go. If we waited any longer it would just get more difficult. So we signed him up, and he was going to start classes the next January.

Meanwhile I was beginning to get a little jealous and wanting to go back to school myself. I was in the Guard now, and had tuition assistance to help pay for my classes and the GI Bill from active duty to help pay some of my bills. I didn't want to go to WyoTech because, after my job search, my being a mechanic in the civilian world didn't seem like a realistic option. So I decided to go to college back home in Oregon. I figured I could start the next fall term in September at the community college in Eugene and then apply to go to the University of Oregon after I was already there.

I'm one of those people who likes to do things right there. So when I finally said, hey, this is what I want to do, I walked into work and gave them all of about a week's notice that I was moving. I resigned my recruiting position and put in for an interstate transfer to the Oregon National Guard. I sold pretty much everything I could to get some extra money; then put the few things I couldn't part with in storage.

John had decided that he would go with me to help me get settled in since he didn't have to leave for school until January. And we headed out, with nothing but his Camaro, my truck, and what we could pack in the back of them.

I listened to a Dora music CD over and over again for almost the entire three-thousand mile trip. We ran into a tornado in Kansas, where we had almost all of our family pictures ruined. But, other than that, the trip went pretty smooth. And about four days later we were in Oregon.

We got an apartment near school and down the street from the National Guard armory. I got myself enrolled in school and transferred to my new unit in Oregon. It was right around the same time that Hurricane Katrina hit and, the day after I transferred units, my new unit was called upon for support.

It wasn't mandatory for me to go; I wasn't even technically on their books yet. But, as is always, I volunteered. I spent just a few weeks in New Orleans. And then the unit sent all the students back first. And I was back, just in time, to start school.

I went to Lane County Community College and Dance was my major. Because I already had my associates in general studies, most of my required classes were completed. And I had a term with nothing but a Theater 101 class and seven different dance classes.

I loved it. It was pretty much the first time that I had danced since I joined the Army. And now I was getting to do it every day. I was starting to get used to my new unit. I saw my family more then I had in the last four years combined. I got Georgia into a really good developmental day care center where she could go during the day after John moved to Wyoming. And I applied to the University of Oregon and to the ROTC program there. I was on a roll and life was perfect... or almost perfect.

As January rolled near, I started thinking about what it would be like to lose John again. For the first time in our marriage, we had now spent one entire year together. I was getting used to it and didn't want to be without him again if I didn't have to be.

I tried to talk him into staying in Oregon; going to the local college for Automotive, or getting a job at one of the trucking companies there. But his heart was set on going to WyoTech. So, once again, after four months in Oregon, I picked up and moved to Wyoming in a last minute decision. This time, I decided, since I was already going to be there, that I would go to WyoTech, too.

I enrolled in the diesel management program and, now, John and I weren't only living together, but going to school together. We were even in the same class. And the way WyoTech worked, you went to one class all the way through before starting the next. So John and I now spent pretty much every hour of every day together.

We got up, dropped off Georgia at preschool, went to school together, went to lunch together, and then went back home for the evening.

It may seem like a lot of time for two people to spend together, but I think we were happier there then we were anywhere else. We were also both doing really well in class. During the Management portion of the Program I had a 99% GPA on a 100% scale, tied with only one other person. Then, when I moved to the power trains portion, I was put in a class leader position, which would have looked really good to all the companies that hire out of there.

John and I were finally back to normal since his return home from Iraq and, once again, it looked like I had a shot at being a mechanic. And then... yes that's right, four months later, John was out four-wheeling with some friends a few days before his birthday, and he got in an accident.

He had hit a jump and, when he went off of it, he went left and the four-wheeler went right. Damage to the four-wheel was minimal, but John broke his collarbone. At first, he didn't know it was broken. So he got back on the four-wheeler, loaded it up in the truck, and drove home.

I took him to the hospital when I found out what happened. Because his break was so bad, he was required to have surgery to put the bones back in place and repair the muscle damage that was done.

We were in the middle of our power trains class, and there was going to be no way for John to finish it. School policy stated that, if he missed over two days, he would be kicked out. And it was going to be months until he was able to recover enough for mechanic work.

Without John's GI Bill, we could not afford to stay in Wyoming, which meant I could not afford to continue to go to school. So once again, Four months later, we moved again; this time going back to Georgia, where we had originally started.

In less than a year, we moved three times, I went to two colleges, saw a whole lot of the country, and were now right back where we started; broke, in debt with student loans for school we had not finished, and had no jobs. The year itself was not wasted. I got to try out both colleges that I wanted to attend before I joined the military, deployed in support of hurricane Katrina and, most importantly, got to spend an entire year with my daughter and my husband (outside of the few weeks I was deployed to Katrina, that is).

It was the first year that we had ever spent together as family without anybody gone, and the most time we had ever spent together.

After we moved back to Georgia, we vowed never to move again. At first, John could not work because of his injury. So I got jobs working both as a waitress at IHOP and as a fleet service technician at U.S. Xpress, the same trucking company that had fired John a year earlier. I worked four ten-hour days at US Xpress and then, anywhere from eight to twelve hours a day, six to seven days a week, at IHOP. I was averaging forty hours a week at U.S. Xpress and sixty hours a week at IHOP, my supposed part-time job.

During all of this, I also had to attend my National Guard duty one weekend a month. But that turned out to be my relief. I would get the weekend off of both jobs, and then only have to be at drill from 0745 to about 1700, getting the entire evening off.

After John got better and could go back to work, he started working for U.S. Xpress again and

I quit my second job at IHOP. I went back to school and continued to stay on at U.S. Xpress. John and I both worked nights on the opposite ends of the week. From time to time, the schedule changed in the hours but, for the most part, I was working from 7 p.m. to 7 a.m. on Sunday through Tuesday and 7 p.m. to 1 a.m. on Wednesday, while he was working 12 p.m. to 6 a.m. on Wednesday and 6 p.m. to 6 a.m. Thursday through Saturday.

This schedule left us with only seeing each other when we came in to go to bed and wake up to go to work. Most of the time we had off during the week was spent either sleeping or at school. So once again, drill weekends continued to be our refuge. It was the one weekend a month when we could see each for more than an hour at a time.

Life was horrible. We made less money than we did in the Army, we never saw each other, and I missed doing what I loved. So, when I found out a unit in my brigade was being deployed, I jumped at the chance to go.

# Saying Good Bye

THE HARDEST PART OF ANY deployment is saying good bye. The first time John left, I didn't wait until he got on the bus. I left early because we knew it would be harder to wait. We kissed and hugged, said our goodbyes, and then he walked me out to the Camaro. I made it less than one block and I began to cry. I ended up pulling over in the parking lot to my motor pool, and sat there and cried until my eyes were clear enough for me to drive home. It took all I had to not go back. I just kept telling myself that it would be worse if I did; that I would be making it harder on him. I cried for three straight days after that, and I spent the next few months wishing I would have stayed until the end, and taken every moment I had with him.

The next time, when he came home on leave and had to return, I remembered how much I wished for those last moments and I stayed until the end. This time, I didn't wait until he was gone to cry. I started before we ever got to the send-off point. I begged and pleaded for him to stay. I know he couldn't, and he had no choice but to go back, but I couldn't help myself. I told him he could refuse, take the discharge, and go AWOL; whatever it took for him to stay home and be there with me and for the birth of our child. He was strong enough to say no, to hug me, and tell me everything was going to be alright, even though we both knew it wasn't.

*16 Sept 08*
*Dear John,*

*You're probably not even on the plane yet, but you've still been gone long enough that I need you to come back. I sat on the sidewalk at the gym for a good 20 minutes until I came home. The only ones there when I left were two guys in BDUs and some gym employees.*

*Part of me just sat there wishing you'd come back, that since you weren't on the manifest list, you couldn't get on the plane and they'd take you back to the gym. The other part of me just didn't want to face the reality of coming home and having you not be there.............I thank God that you came home and I got to spend the time with you I did. I need to remember to be thankful for it, and not be hostile that they sent you back.*

*It's said that absence makes the heart grow fonder, but it just doesn't seem possible to be any more in love with you then I already am. I often wonder if anyone has felt as lucky as I do.*

*You make my world worth living. I'm not sure how I ever got along without you.*
*Forever Yours,*
*Jenna Jaye*

.

I try to blame the fact that I was so emotional,

and that it was so hard, on the fact that I was pregnant and it must have been hormones. But I wasn't the only one that cried. My husband cried for the first few days he was back in the country. He never told me how hard it was for him, I think, because he wanted to be strong for me. But Hardman, from my unit, ran into him while he was in Baghdad waiting to fly to Fallujah. He told me that he saw my husband sitting outside with his head in his hands crying. My husband told him everything was okay, but he knew different. When I asked my husband about it later on, he admitted that he cried for several days after going back to Iraq.

When he was gone, I had the selfish view; that he had gotten to go to Iraq and was with his friends over there while I was left behind all alone. It wasn't until I finally got deployed that I realized I was only trying to go on living my normal life without him in it, but he was trying to live each day not only without me, but without getting to be there for our daughter. I was missing him, but he was missing out on us.

When my turn came, I was sad, but was doing okay, at first, because I was looking forward to finally going to Iraq and serving my time. John, however, was not. Our tables had turned back the first time he left. He dropped me off at the airport and left early, remembering how hard it was when we tried to stay together until the end. He kissed me good bye, walked out of the building, crying before he even made it to the car.

This time, we tried to make it easier. So, instead, we split our separate ways and said goodbye about an hour before it was time for me to get on the bus. We tried to act like it was no big deal; just another day at work. That way, we weren't showing how upset we were to our daughter. It was the first time that one of us had left and neither of us had cried. Some may think that's because it gets easier. But I don't think that is so. Knowing that you are going to go another year before you see each other again, and that you're going to miss all the important things, never gets easier. Instead, it's like you just get better at hiding it in front of other people... and even a little to yourself.

I didn't cry for almost a month after I left this time. Not because I didn't miss my family, but because I couldn't. I would sit in my top bunk, sad and depressed, thinking about my family and all the stuff I was missing; always to the point of getting ready to just completely break down. But a tear never left my eyes. I told John it must have been because I left my heart at home with him and Georgia.

# McGregor Range

WE LEFT FOR MCGREGOR RANGE, New Mexico on June 12th, 2007. It's a small training camp outside of Fort Bliss, Texas, and it's currently home to some fourteen-hundred-plus troops preparing to deploy to Iraq. There are people here from the National Guard in Georgia, Ohio, Kansas, and Texas, as well as us. In addition to them, we also have a large group of Air Force and Navy soldiers here training for the same mission; to run a prison camp in Umm Qasr.

There is a prison camp in Umm Qasr, which is in southern Iraq just north of the Kuwait border, called Camp Bucca. It's the largest detainee facility in Iraq, currently holding upwards of nineteen thousand troops. Each unit will be tasked and assigned to different duties. Some were assigned to guard the detainees, others to run convoy operations, and then some to help run the base.

Our training consists of everything from weapons qualification, first aid, and NBC (Nuclear, Biological, and Chemical) training that you get on a regular basis throughout your time in the military, to doing security operations, riot control, detainee operations, close hand-to-hand combat, and language labs. Some of the training seems repetitive and boring, especially to some of our guys who just returned from Iraq last fall. Some of the training is good for us to have. I emphasize *some*.

The worst part is that a lot of it is dragged out, and some of the people have more training in the areas of instruction then the instructors, but they're still forced to sit through it. In addition to that, we are treated like basic training privates, even E-7s and E-8s, upper level NCO's, who often have twenty-plus years of military experience. And it's fully due to the fact that we're National Guard. We aren't allowed off our training camp, except for what they call *green days*, which simply means a day off. And, even then, we are only allowed to go to the main post. We're not allowed to drink, wear civilian clothes, or even talk to the active Army. We have to sign out on a roster if we go to the gym or the Post Exchange (PX). To make it worse, many of our instructors talk down to us and give us little to no respect.

I'll admit it. When I was on active duty, I looked down on the Guard like they were part-time soldiers and worthless. During Iraq, things have changed, though. Guard and Reserve don't sit on the sidelines. They make up a large number of the troops deployed. Most Guard troops I've met have made just as many, and often even more, deployments then regular Army soldiers.

Like I said, though, some of the training has

been good. Our hand-to-hand combat classes are things that can be used not just if the situation arises over there, but also in real life. Shortly after having the defensive class and learning different pressure points, I was in a training exercise that involved me keeping control of the "detainee." I had one hand holding his shoulder to try to keep control and, when he attempted to go for my 9mm pistol, I automatically reached over for a pressure point in his neck to get him off me and put him down.

We also were required to go through CLS, or Combat Life Saver, class. This is a class where you get into first aid tactics for the battlefield; a lot of the things we get in regular first aid but, in addition, we gave IV's and learned how to treat for several other injuries that have long names I can't spell. The best thing about that class is that they broke down for us the different types of injuries we often encounter in combat and the percent of them. So we could see just how important it was for us to know some of the different things. Most units have a percentage between ten percent and fifty percent who are CLS certified. Our unit had over ninety percent.

Other good training classes and field exercises we had were language, convoy operations, and room clearing. My favorite part was getting to qualify with the .50 caliber machine gun. It was the first time I had every gotten to qualify with one, and it just so happened to be the 4th of July. I got to fire twice because of a weapons malfunction, so I got to fire over three hundred rounds. I considered it to be my fireworks for the day.

On my birthday we had convoy operations, and I got to put over seven hundred rounds downrange by way of an M249. They set off makeshift IEDs, broke down some vehicles, and had people firing at us with AK47s (blanks of course). The purpose was to be able to react to the situations in a seven-vehicle convoy element.

Even though all the rounds are blanks and can't hurt you, it still becomes a stressful environment because different people are yelling to do different things. It was really good training because you got to see how well the other people reacted to the different situations, behaved under stress, and just how well they worked together.

The only training that I really hated (I mean, *really* hated) was when we got sprayed with OC. It's like a pepper spray. They spray it right across your eyes. Then you go down a lane where you're required to take down and fight different "detainees." The purpose of the training is help you build confidence and to let you know that, if you get sprayed in a situation, you can still proceeded with the mission. I have no doubt that anyone who truly needed to could continue the mission, though, without the aforementioned exercise. To me, it's kind of like saying that you have to be shot with a rifle to carry it.

*21 July 07*
*Dear John,*

*I've never felt so much pain in my entire life as I did today. It started with yesterday, we did defensive tactics. Things like holds, pressure points, & wrist locks. I got into a makeshift ring with four instructors who beat the tar out of me, took a massive blow to the chest, got my wrist almost snapped, and got a blow to the legs so hard it made me fall straight to the ground. And I handled all I of it like a champ, but to say when they sprayed us, I cried like the little girl that I am.*

*I went up and got sprayed. I thought I was done so I ducked down and shook it off, leaned up and opened my eyes all the way, let it drip in a little but, thought I was good to go and then they told me they didn't get me all the way and I had to do it again.*

*I was so mad I started yelling "you got me, you got me, you F\*\*\*ing got me." And then they made me close my eyes and do it again/ after the second spray that was it I was done. I started going down the lane, and kept my composure as I put the first guy down. As I was on my way to the second guy all I remember was them telling me to open my eyes and me yelling I can't and then starting to bawl. I was crying and screaming through the whole thing. When I had to use my baton to strike, I was swinging hard enough to takes someone's head off. At least it felt like it.*

*It was by far the worst experience of my life. Afterwards I was crying, "Please, make it stop. Make it go away." fully well knowing no one could do anything about it. I hung onto whatever was standing next to me, seeking comfort, just wishing it was you.*

*I've broken my femur, had a kid, and this was by far the worst thing I've ever gone through. I love you and I miss you so much. I wish you could have been there. Lord knows I needed you.*

*Love,*

*Jenna Jaye*

*P.S. Afterward, the other two girls told me it was nice to see me cry, because now they know I'm human. And yes, I cried like a baby, but I finished the whole thing, and there were grown men crying right there with me.*

During that block of instruction we had numerous injured within our battalion; many bearable, just aches and bruises. But we had one who got get his wrist broke, and another get his knee cap dislocated. That individual ended up having to have surgery and couldn't deploy with us for medical reasons. By the time our training was over, we lost so many Army people that we were almost unable to deploy.

I agree with most of the training we received and understand its usefulness. But by injuring soldiers during training we reduce our deployable force and lessen our Army's combat effectiveness.

# Arriving In Country

BETWEEN OUR MOBILIZATION STATION and our assigned duty station in Iraq, all units go through Kuwait. We first stopped in Bangor, Maine, and then in Leipzig, Germany. Including the refueling stops, the whole flight time was about eighteen hours. We arrived at about 2100 hours but, after unloading the plane, taking the bus to our transition camp, and getting in-processed, it was about 0200 hrs before we got to our tents to lie down.

While I, myself, have never been to Kuwait, I looked at my friend and made a comment about how I feel almost at home. It's a different base, and even a different country, but it feels and looks the same as the bases in Iraq and I just felt like I was right at home. When I made the comment to him, I thought he'd think I was strange, but he felt the same way. Like many other people in our group, he had not only been to Iraq before, but had been through this same base in Kuwait several times.

As some of the others walked by who had been here with him before, he asked them all how they felt being back there. All their comments were almost the same. They said they felt strangely comfortable here. And most of them didn't like that it felt that way.

Outside of all the returning soldiers, all the new soldiers mainly just complained about the heat. I won't say it's not hot. It is. The best way to describe it is having a blow-dryer stuck in your face. But it's also not anywhere near as hot as it gets. It's been around 120 degrees while we there , and I remember it getting up in the low 130's last time I was t/here. I've been lucky enough to miss the summers, though, always arriving in late August. Several others here have experienced 140-plus degrees. Those pictures you see where troops took a picture of the thermometer in the shade reading 135 degrees from what I understand, that's the normal summer heat.

We stayed in Kuwait for about a week. We had a few in processing briefs; did a test-fire on our weapons. But mainly, we just sat around waiting on a flight out of here to our base in Iraq. In that time, we mainly just got acclimated to the time and temperature. I, myself, hid in the air conditioned tent; coming out only to eat and after the sun went down. I know that acclimating myself to the temperature is important. But it was almost fall, and that means the temperature was going to start going down. So I intended to get the least of it as possible.

We got to visit the various little shops and stores that they have on base. Jewelry shops and gift shops, as well as several fast food stands from back in the states. Most bases, other than small FOBs, have some form of a Burger King or Pizza

Hut. But Kuwait has many more than the bases in Iraq. At Bucca, they had a Green Bean (which is like the military version of Starbucks), Burger King, Subway, and Pizza Hut. In Kuwait they have all of those plus a steak house, an oriental place, Baskin Robbins, Starbucks, KFC, and Taco Bell. So anyone who was deployed to Kuwait and says they had it rough; just laugh. Outside of having to use port-a-johns and having smoldering heat, this place pretty much has all the comforts of back home.

# The Eternal Struggle

A FRIEND RECENTLY ASKED ME if I regret volunteering. The answer was yes and no. The mommy part of me thinks I'm an in idiot; that there is a perfect little girl at home waiting for me. I'm missing out on her growing up; and there will be moments which I will never get back. My husband missed her birth, her first smile, and her first Christmas. I've already missed the first time she tried to hold the spoon and feed herself, her first birthday, and the first present she opened. By the time this deployment is over, I will have missed yet another birthday, her first ballet class, and quite possibly her first day of kindergarten. I won't be there to teach her to read or to ride a bike. I can no longer read her stories and kiss her goodnight. I can't bake cookies with her or even take her for ice cream when it's hot out.

The same day I found out we got our orders and that we were finally leaving, Georgia fell asleep with me in my bed watching cartoons. After she fell asleep, I laid there crying because I had already begun to miss her. Things like that make me regret it. They make me regret that I volunteered for Iraq and, sometimes, that I ever even came back in after I got out the first time.

But as much as I want to just tell the military to go to hell and stay home, I want just as much to be here and to do my part. I want to serve my country and go to bed knowing that I didn't make someone else take my place. I want my daughter to know that I did something with my life and that I was a part of something bigger than myself.

When she grows up and reads the history books, I want her to know that I was there and to be proud of me. And that's where the eternal struggle lies. To do what I love, what makes me happy, and what makes me feel proud and, in doing so, give up moments with my daughter that I can never get back. Or to get completely out, work a regular job that gives me no sense of satisfaction and no sense of pride, but never have to worry about missing a moment of my daughter's life: knowing that I can be there and be the mother that she needs and deserves.

I'm lucky to have a daughter who has been able to handle this so well. When I talk to her on the phone, she gets excited and will tell me about her day and that she loves me and misses me. But then, when she's ready to get off the phone, she says "Okay, mommy, you go back to work now." and then hangs up or gives the phone back to John. Sometimes it's hard when she doesn't want to talk for long, because it reminds me that I'm not a normal part of her everyday life. But, at the same time, it makes me happy to know she's doing okay without me.

For me, being a soldier is more than a job. It is who I am. I won *Solider of the Year* for my battalion, and then for my brigade. I competed for *Solider of the Year* for the state of Tennessee, and we had to write an essay about why we're in the Tennessee National Guard. I've never really adapted to being a Guard soldier. I still just consider myself Army. But this is what I wrote:

*"I am an American soldier. I am a warrior and a member of a team. I serve the people of the United States and live the Army values. These words are the first lines in the Soldier's Creed and are, by far, the words that best exemplify who I am and why I serve.*

*I joined the Army for the same reasons as a lot of people; money for college, a job, adventure, independence. I had pride in the fact that I was doing something for myself and on my own. Soon after joining, September 11th hit, and with it came a new outlook. I couldn't tell anybody what I did for a living without having them say thank you, or telling me a story when they, or someone they loved, were in the service. It made me feel like I was part of something bigger then myself. ...For me, being a solider is not only what I am, but who I am. I am the Guardian of freedom and the American way of life. I am an American Soldier."*

I can recite the Soldier's Creed in my sleep. When I'm having a bad day or questioning life, it's what I say to make me feel better. The words *"I am an*

*American soldier"* have the ability, themselves, to remind me that my life has meaning and purpose, and that I matter.

I try often to think of new things I can do at home, new jobs that I might enjoy, that would get me away from the military life. I tell myself I've served my time, I did my part, and now it's time to let someone else serve theirs while I go home and take care of my family. But no matter how many times I say it, it just doesn't work.

There's always a mission somewhere. Something that needs to get done and that someone will have to do. And I can't imagine myself ever being that someone that would turn it down. I'm in the Guard because I decided that, as much as I love the Army and wish I was full time, the National Guard will allow me to be home with my family and then go out when I'm needed. To me it's a good compromise. It gives me some of both worlds. But no matter what I choose, I'll never be satisfied.

Anytime I'm out with the military, I can't help think that it takes time away from me being at home. And any time I'm at home and hear the TV, I feel bad that I'm not there helping out with the rest of them. There are so many people who have spouses and kids, who wish they could be at home, yet they volunteered to come here just as I did. I think that, what I refer to as my eternal struggle, is also a struggle for many others here.

# Being a Female

LIKE ANY JOB, THERE ARE things about my job that I dislike. And like any other male-dominated field, there are things to overcome. There are people who think that you're incapable; that you're not an equal; people who treat you poorly; people who will not give you a fair shot. It's normal and I've come to expect it.

On active duty, when I first reported to my motor pool, I was looked at like another useless female mechanic; one of those girls who probably took the job so they could work with a bunch of guys. And, of course, it didn't help that pretty much the only thing I knew about being a mechanic was what I was taught in my AIT school. But I overcame it.

When I first got there, I was tasked to work with soldiers who would help me learn my way around the motor pool and teach me more about my job. When we got assigned to a vehicle, I always made a point to jump right in and, whenever I had trouble or found out I didn't know something, I asked. I took advantage of every chance I had to learn and make myself a better mechanic.

I tried very hard not be another stereotypical female mechanic like they had dealt with who didn't work and didn't try. I volunteered for every outside job and mission that came up and, after I started working on my own equipment, I would often work through lunch to finish a job. Eventually, my efforts paid off, and my fellow mechanics saw me as "just one of the guys" if you will.

Occasionally, we got a new guy in the motor pool and, to start with, most of them didn't like me at first. But, for the most part, they all came around, with a few exceptions, of course.

I can't say I blame them for their attitudes towards women. The longer I was there, the more I began to join them and think the same way. I had a female E-6 who was very seldom seen actually working. And, when she did, she often did more damage than good. A person at that rank should be extremely proficient in their job. There was no doubt in my mind, or anyone else's, that she got her rank solely because of her sex, and I resented it. She was an NCO, but she never took care of her soldiers, and she would have to use a technical manual to change the oil.

In addition to her, I had two other females who did not know their job and could only assist someone else in repairs; never do them alone. One of them was assigned to help me one day and, at the first chance she got, she slid away to hide in the back of a trailer and go to sleep. As hypocritical as it may seem, I began to hate women in the motor pool just as much as anyone else did. I took that position that any female was worthless until they proved to me otherwise, just as I had also had to do before.

When I got attached to the unit I am currently with, I encountered the same issues. This time, it proved to be different, though. I was instantly put in a headquarters unit because I was a female. I didn't like it, but it was a part of life. We were in training, so I didn't have the same opportunities to prove myself through my work. But I still continued to volunteer for any extra duties and work as hard as I could. Eventually I started to get the nicknames "Killer" and "Hardcore." They were joking when they said it, but they came about because of my attitude toward things. And they were a good thing. It made me feel like I was once again proving that I could work and be treated like the rest of them. I tried to get into one of the line platoons, but was still unable to. I had found a platoon sergeant who would take me. But command would not let me go because I was a female.

While I was still having some issues, I did feel like I was beginning to get respected and overcome them. I was in a field artillery unit, which is an all male unit, and I just felt like I was going to have to work harder until I got to Iraq.

When I got there, the company's line platoons went to work in the detainee camp, and headquarters personnel resumed their normal functions. I was sent to work in the TOC, the Tactical Operations Center, where I sit manning a phone that never rings in case something happened. My evenings mainly consist of watching movies and playing computer games. Since I've been in this unit, I have been routinely put in positions in which I am completely useless, which leaves me both unable to prove my worth and obtain a better position.

I tried to get out of my job behind the desk, and out to the compound where the rest of the soldiers worked. I didn't think it would happen but I still tried. Before, it was our command that was keeping me from joining one of the platoons. So I began to make the arguments to them. It almost worked. One of our first sergeants (oddly enough, our company has two) asked both platoon sergeants if they had anyone they wanted to trade out. He was going to replace me. The platoon sergeants told him no. He told me this and said, "Sorry. I guess they didn't have anyone they wanted to get rid of…" and then, right after that, he said "…or they just didn't want a girl out there." I came to find out it was the latter of the two options.

*22 Sept 07*
*Dear John,*

*I finally got them to admit I'm only in my position because I'm a girl. I know I told you about Top trying to get me into the compound and out of my current job. Well I asked one of the platoon sergeants about it, to see if he was telling me the truth. He was. The Platoon sergeant I asked didn't even try to tell me it was because he didn't want to lose one his guys. He just came out and said it was because I was a female.*

*I respect that he told me the truth and because of it I have no hard feelings towards him about it, but it still doesn't help my situation.*

*I love what I do, I love being a soldier, and I was raised to work hard, but I'm never going to get that chance being in this unit. People keep trying to tell me to be happy; that I have an easy job where I don't have to anything, but I can't. I'm in the military because I volunteered. I'm in Iraq because I volunteered. To me this isn't something that I was made to do. I'm not here waiting to get out when my time is up. This is my career, but I'm never going to be able to make something out of it, out of myself if I'm not given the opportunity.*

*I'm at a loss now of what to do. For the first time I feel like the worthless soldiers I hate. I wish you were here so bad. I wish I was deployed with my old unit. I wish I had NCOs that gave a s\*\*t about their troops. I love you so much. I'm sorry if I'm ever in a bad mood or mean when I call home, but this place and these people have taken away all of my morale.*

*I love you,*
*Jenna Jaye*

Sometimes I feel like there's no way to get over the stigma of being a female. That no matter how hard you work or what you do, it will never completely go away.

Two nights ago, I came across a guy who I had found out was telling people he had slept with me. I had never met him before, nor even saw him until the other night when I came across him. When I realized who he was, I made a point of stopping him and telling him what I thought of it. In doing so, I may have also, incidentally, threatened to take a k-bar to his neck. I knew it probably wasn't the smartest thing to say but, in my mind, threatening him beat out the other option of just straight out punching him.

Needless to say, the incident got back to my command, and I was talked to about it. I knew it would happen, and I knew I would be told I should have filed a formal complaint. But how am I supposed to. I have enough trouble being a female in my unit. Filing a complaint would only further illustrate that fact. I'm told to keep a battle buddy, someone I trust to hang out with and walk around with. It's kind of a support system in the military, staying in pairs to keep you safe. Females are limited, especially when it comes to finding one to go the same place as you and do whatever it is you need to, so I usually have a male. This is expected because of our limits in males. My assigned battle buddy for going to and from work is even a male. But as soon as I'm seen walking around with a member of the opposite sex, there are automatically assumptions that there must be a relationship between the two of us.

Any decent looking female under the age of 40 seen talking to a guy more than once is automatically assumed to have a relationship of a sexual nature with them. People talk and begin to spread rumors, no matter what the situation. On top of that, there are always the guys who think it is high school and write obscene things on walls about what they would like to see or do to you in bathrooms. And, when it happens, often it begins to affect other perceptions about you. Whether the comments hold merit or not, if you're talked about in such a manner, there must be a reason.

There are those people who will stick up for you. They will defend you against rumors and mark out the stuff they see on walls, but they never win out. The people who make comments and start rumors always seem to prevail.

My entire career has consisted of me trying to work hard and overcome the stigma of being a girl. And, for the first time, I feel like I've failed. I'm not naive. I know I'll never be Infantry, be Special Forces, or be a Ranger. But I don't want to be given a special job or special treatment. I just want to be treated like everybody else; have the same chances to succeed; and the same chances to fail. I want to go to sleep every day knowing that I worked as hard as I could and did as much as I could. I want to wake up every morning knowing that I'm going to do it again; that I will give it my all. That's why I love the military. It allows me to challenge myself and my perception of myself. But times like this, when I go to bed feeling useless and worthless, when I wake up knowing that I'm going to have another day where I don't matter and I won't be able to make anything out of myself; I feel like my whole career has been a waste. That everything I want to be and have worked so hard to become has just been pointless and that I should find something else.

# Polite, Professional, and Prepared To Kill

EVENTUALLY, I GOT WHAT I wanted, and I went out to work in the compound. Our company was required to task out people to work with a different unit, and I was one of the ones sent. The compound was what they called the "super max," i.e. the maximum security compound. There weren't a lot of differences between it and a normal compound, outside of the number of people that were there. It had, maybe, a quarter of the number of the other compounds, all of which were divided up evenly into smaller groups.

The training we got for our mobilization led me to a much different impression of what working in the compound would be like. Even in the super max, there was rarely any trouble from the detainees. I'm not saying they were angels. One compound started a riot and burned down their towers. Others would throw rocks. And, in some compounds, they would kill another detainee and then drop him at the front gate. But those were things that only happened from time to time, and the events were spread over the different compounds. There wasn't just one group who rioted every day and had mass slayings. For the most part we thought of ourselves as babysitters. We made sure they ate, had lots of water, took them to the doctor, and made them clean up after themselves. We even played the radio for them in the evening and gave them a soccer ball. We considered ourselves to be the *Camp Bucca Day Care* staff.

For the most part, we were polite and courteous to them. There were always the few who thought they were Billy Bad Ass and had to act like a jerk. But the majority of the people talked to the detainees like normal people as long as they weren't giving them any problems. One day, we were escorting detainees to another compound. One of the guys was yelling at the detainees to put his eyes down. Then he looked over and noticed another detainee that appeared to be in pain. It was an older man, with back issues, having trouble trying to sit in the manner he was required to. The solider got the interpreter and asked the detainee if he needed a chair, water, or anything else to make him more comfortable. He was truly concerned.

It was then that I remembered a phrase I heard while I was at McGregor; *Polite, Professional, and Prepared to Kill*. It truly explains how we must behave while doing this job and while serving in this county.

Whenever I have to ask a detainee to shut the gate so that I can lock it, or to get the chief, I always say thank you. I smile and, when possible, I always ask them to do something before I tell them they have to do it. I try to treat them like normal human beings, with dignity and respect, but I wouldn't hesitate for a moment to shoot one, be it to save my life, a fellow soldier's life, or even the life of another detainee. If the situation called for it, I would pull the trigger without pause.

There are several detainees in the compounds who have done nothing wrong, and are only there because they were in the wrong place at the wrong time. But it's impossible to tell which are which from just looking at them. We treat them all with respect, because it's the best way to keep them from rioting and causing problems, but we must also assume that they are all conspiring to escape or harm one of us. The whole situation really does seem like a paradox some times.

The motto that the Army keeps trying to instill in us is that we're here to "win the hearts and minds of the Iraqi People." In part, I like it, because it's kind of like saying we're here to help. But, at the same time, the statement seems utterly ridiculous because, if we're trying to win them over, we're sure going about it the wrong way.

At least half of the people we have in there are probably completely innocent of any wrong doing. Some end up there because they have neighbors that don't like them. So they will call and give false intelligence so as to get them arrested. Others detainees that are in there unjustly are the ones I said were in the wrong place at the wrong time. When the military gets reports of Intel, or an IED goes off, and the Marines go in to investigate it, they will round up every male within a certain age range and just haul him in, thus landing the individuals here with us. We have courts here that are set up to help release people, but we're still taking in more than we let out. And it takes a very long time to complete the process.

One story I heard about when I first got here was a young man, in his early twenties or so. He worked for the US when the war first began. He made friends with troops on his base and, when the troops were getting ready to leave, they gave the Iraqi a present. They felt bad that he only had sandals to wear. So, as a way of showing their appreciation and as a gesture of good will, they gave the man a pair of combat boots. About six months or so later, soldiers from a different unit did a sweep of their town and noticed the Iraqi wearing combat boots. They arrested the man and brought him to Camp Bucca, where he sat for three years until he was just finally paroled.

Weird stories where people get unjustly arrested happened back in the states, too. But they don't usually end up landing a man in prison for three years without any kind of trial or evidence. And they don't happen every day like they do here.

It's hard, sometimes, knowing that so many of them could be innocent and in prison for no reason, sitting and sleeping right next to the people who have tried to kill us. I find myself looking at them while I'm on guard duty, wondering just which ones are which. I see one and try to imagine if he was the kind of person who would try to shank me he first chance he got, or is he just trying to get by and deal with everything until he can get home. I wonder if we are really helping or, if by putting them together, we are just creating more enemies.

I watch them from the tower each day. My job is to keep an eye on them and to report any suspicious activity, attempts at escape, and make sure that there are not any problems among them. Most of their time is spent in prayer and studying the Kuran. They exercise every day by running and walking around the compound. Some even do pushups and sit ups. They eat their meals in large groups of people, like sitting around a dinner table. I have even seen them teaching one another to read and write.

Just recently we started to work with ICOs, Iraqi Correction Officers. They sit in the tower with us, as well as work in the other positions and jobs. Like the detainees, I often wonder which ones are good and which ones are bad. Most are there because the pay is good for them. Some of them like American's, some don't. Some donot care either way. And probably, at least one or more hates us and is planning our demise. So far, we have been able to make friends with them. They teach us Arabic and we teach them English. We talk a lot about our families and who has how many kids, mainly because that's the most we know how to say to each other. They perform a lot of the same duties and work with us side by side. But no matter how nice they are and how much we may even like them, you can never let yourself fully trust one because there is that possibility that he is there for the sole purpose of gaining intel, or trying to kill you.

*19 Nov 07*
*Dear Mom,*

*Today I was reminded of why I am here, what we are doing, and why I wanted to come back and help be a part of it.*

*We work with Iraqi Correction officers in our job. We call them ICO's for short. We have only just begun to start working with them, but so far they seem to be okay people. Our unit was a little worried at first about how they would receive me, since I was a female, but so far it has been okay. I am learning to say a few words in Arabic, and today we taught some of them a few different pressure points and moves for hand to hand combat. It's not part of our job, but it helps us pass the time and interact with each other in a positive manner.*

*Today while we were talking, one of the guys asked him if he liked Americans. The detainee said yes, and then proceeded to tell him why. He said when Sadam was last in power that they had no food, and trouble finding jobs. Since then, he has gotten a good paying job, his kids now finally are able to go to* school, and they have things like cars and phones that they didn't have before.

When he was telling me this you could tell how much life had improved for him by the way he acted. He told me "Before, no job, no food, for anybody. Now there are jobs, food. My kids go to school. And everyone have car. I have car my dad have car." Things we consider every day staples, they are just now beginning to have.

As ICO's they earn only $500 dollars a month, but for them it is enough to feed their families. Many of them take care of their family and then their brothers as well.

Meeting people like this, whose lives have improved and are glad we are here. That's why I volunteered to come here, to come back. As much as I don't agree with the war, we are doing a lot of good things here. The army is responsible for building schools, hospitals, and roads. They provide jobs and have improved the economy ten fold here.

I miss my family terribly, but when I think about what I am a part of, and how much a difference it can make, it makes me be proud to be here. I know not all the Iraqis like us, that's why we're still getting shot at and we're still here, but hopefully through education and knowledge that will one day change. If not, then in ten years from now we will just be back here again.

I love you and miss you guys,
I'll be home soon,
Jenna

A few days after getting the ICOs, I had my first riot. There had been some others at nearby compounds, but I was working in the TOC when they happened. This time, a compound about three hundred yards away rioted and, soon after, our compound's detainees started throwing "Chi Rocks," which are basically just really hard rocks, but they're made from sand and chi, which is tea. The ICO I had was enthused to be there and help. He held up a shield in front of the wire fencing that served as my towers cage/window and yelled for the chief while they hammered him with rocks. He never tried to duck down or hide, he covered me when I fired back, and stood next to me until the riot was over. For the time being, it was no different than having another soldier in my tower.

# Desensitized

AROUND 2200 LAST NIGHT, I came home from work. I sat down on my bed, turned on my laptop and Yahoo Messenger, and began to talk to my husband. But, just as I said hello, I heard several little explosions. They seemed quieter than the normal mortars. I opened up the door to see if we had gotten hit or not, and saw everyone else at their door doing the same. Just then, we heard one sing right over our heads and it was actually close enough that everyone hit the deck, then got up and went running for the bunker.

I hollered in at my roommate. And she jumped out of bed and headed for the bunker, still in her underwear. Running was not something we normally did, but having a mortar land so close was not the norm either.

Soon after we got to the bunker, the mortars stopped and, as usual, we all came out before we got the okay. The alarm was still sounding and several of the Air Force guys who were new were asking us how long we had been here and what they were supposed to do. Calmly exiting the bunker and walking back to my room, I told them they were supposed to stay there until the alarm ceased and they called an amber status.

Prior to the *all clear*, we had already returned to our rooms to grab our gear, with the attitude that *man, this sucks*. Not because we were mortared, but because we had to go sit in our company areas and wait for the all clear, which was usually a few hours. To us, the mortar attacks were no more than an annoyance that interfered with whatever we might have been doing at the time.

Annoyed, I grabbed my text books with hope that I could at least sit down and get some work done and made my way to the meeting point. Upon arrival, I found out that the mortar we had heard go directly over our heads landed on the other side of the Hesco barrier next to the males' pods. Our meeting area was less than thirty meters from where it had struck.

Shortly thereafter, we were notified that there were seven wounded and one KIA from the attack. My first response, "It's about time they hit something." Then, when we were released, I turned around, went back to my pod, and treated it like any other day. Later, I found out it was a civilian contractor, and my attitude didn't change. I was telling John about it, and when he said something along the lines of "Oh, my god" and then "Man, that sucks," my response was, "Oh well, they volunteered just like the rest of us."

The first response of one of the guys, when

they found out that it was a third country national that was the indvidual killed, was "Man, I hope it's not the guys who makes the fries at Burger King." Then, just a few hours later, everyone including the TCNs, were back at work, doing their normal jobs and acting like nothing had happened. Minus a few of our guys who had to pull some pieces of skull off the top of their chew and pieces of shrapnel out of their living area  no more thought or concern was given to it.

I know that it had to affect certain people; especially those who went to aid after it hit and who had to help clean up the aftermath. But having a person die seemed no more troubling then if we had hit a stray animal in the road.

Neither my responses nor theirs were out of disregard for life but, basically, the only way to function normally in a place like this is to accept it as an everyday possibility and go on like normal. We are in a pretty good area as far as not having a lot of incidents but, when something does happen, it seems to impact us no more than if we were to see our buddy drop a weight at the gym. We would feel bad about his broken foot, but would probably just rag on him for doing something that stupid.

We learn to expect the worst, and mentally we prepare for it by detaching ourselves. To be effective and be able to complete our missions, no matter what they are, we can't let anything affect us. It's why we return home and seem different. We live our lives removed from the ones we love in a completely different state of mind, geared solely towards our mission, because, without it, most of us would never make it over there for a year at a time.

# Comradery

THERE ARE FEW PLACES IN this world that you will find the friendships and comradery that exist in the military. The amount of time that you spend with other soldiers in your platoon and your squad is immense. You train together, work together and often even live together. You depend on each other for support and entrust each other with your lives. From the day you reach basic training, you are taught the battle buddy system and to always keep someone with you.

There are many people in the military with whom I have shared my life and will never forget, and this deployment was no exception. From my roommates, to my battle buddies, the people in my squad, and soldiers that I met from other units, I have had a number of people who have made an impact on me throughout the year.

On active duty, the person who I could always trust and count on was my friend, Dan Hardman. We were fellow soldiers and friends. He taught me a lot about being a mechanic and was always there to take care of me. He even punched out a guy on my behalf once. On this deployment, the people who I came to know and trust seem to be never ending. I made friends from other states and units and even managed to make a friend with an Air Force solider who lived across from me.

There was Adams, who used to spend hours on end walking with me on roving guard, and talking about life and everything under the sun. He was just twenty-one and, while that's only three years younger than me, I used to tease him about being a teenager. It would have been easy to see him as my little brother but, in all honestly, as well collected and together as he was, he was probably more like my big brother.

Cain was my sanity. We sat on the porch (really just my front steps) and talked about life almost every night for the last few months I was there. When I first met him, I saw him as the quiet type but, as I got to know him, I found out that he was as "out there" as me. We complained about our unit and the Army together; about how messed up it was and how much we hated it. But both of us wanted to stay in for hopes that we may one day be able to help fix it.

Everyone always joked that, if Cain wasn't complaining, he wasn't happy. But, in addition to his non-complacent attitude, he was also every-one's comic relief. He was known for his "sumo diaper" and dancing with a mop. Once, we even managed to get him into a pair of pink thongs.

There were a few others, too; ones who I can't name, simply because I'm not sure what happened to them after we returned and, since I can't get a hold of them, I can't get permission to use their names in this book. Named or not, they were my friends. They made the difference in me being sane and surviving the trip. They were there when I missed my family and when the only thing I wanted to do was go home.

The closest relationship of all, though, was probably a guy by the name of Carmen. We met because he was friends with one of my roommates. They had worked at the same compound. He turned into my boxing coach and then, eventually, my tutor.

We both took classes and, even though we both had other military goals, we would always yell at the other person for considering doing anything other than finish their degree first.

Carmen was the one person who I ever really had meaningful conversations with. We could talk about education and politics. He taught me about the stock market and I managed to crack his nose one day in the ring (probably only because he had already gotten it cracked in a fight a few weeks earlier, but I still like to take credit for it). He reminded me that I could be anything; and that all I had to do was try.

All in all, the people I met on this deployment

will be unforgettable. We were there for each other when family passed away and shared cigars when babies were born. We consoled the ones who got divorced and gave hell to the ones who got married. Even though we couldn't take part in the events that were happening at home, we shared them with each other in our own way in Iraq. We spend years on deployment and away from our families, with nobody to talk to and be there for us except each other.

I know, when the deployment is over, that I will never see many of these people again, and sometimes it saddens me. There will be no more evening smokes with Cain, no more Subway with my Hawaiian truck driver, or boxing practices with Carmen. I won't get to joke around with Adams, or give the set of brothers in my platoon hell. My hardcore ex-Special Forces buddy won't be around to cheer me on and remind me that I'm as good as all the guys. We say we will call and stay in touch, visit when we're in town, but there will only be a few of us who actually do. We will talk a few times here and there, and try to stay in touch at first. But, eventually, the conversations will lessen. And eventually they will fade away.

# Army VS Guard

IT MAY SOUND WEIRD BECAUSE I voluntarily left my home and my family to go to another country for a year, but if I could do anything, I would like to be a stay-at-home mom. I'd like to be the mom who is there; standing at the end of the driveway everyday when the children get off the bus. The one who makes a big homemade dinner every night and always has dessert to go with it. I'd like to spend my summer taking my kids to the pool. And every fall, I'd sew their Halloween costumes.

A lot of this idea is largely impracticable due to the fact that, these days, it costs too much to live for me to not work and to stay home. The other part is that I love being in the military. I am a goal-oriented person, and the military just fits me. There was always something to work towards, the next promotion, or getting the next school. I didn't spend every day doing the same repetitive job. Most of my time was spent on line in the motor pool fixing trucks. But every Thursday we had field training. And then there were always ranges to go to and different tasks and training that came up. Everyone has that perfect job, the one that makes them happy and look forward to going to work each day; and for me that job is the Army. Unfortunately, it's not perfect for my family.

I'm not saying now that Army life is bad for family life. In fact, I believe the total opposite. One of the benefits of the Army is the amount of time you get off to spend with your family. We get thirty days of paid leave plus an average of one four-day weekend a month. We always got off at 1500 hrs on Thursdays for family time, and there was never an issue if you had to bring your child to the doctor or go to their school. I don't know about other places but, in my battalion, attending parent/teacher conferences was mandatory.

It's not like a civilian job, where you have to clock out and worry about your paycheck being deducted. When I had my daughter, and my husband was deployed, there were a few times where I even brought Georgia to work with me. It wasn't an everyday thing, but there were times when the babysitter was sick or had another engagement. I set up a playpen in one of the spare offices and would sit down and go to work. As long as my job was accomplished, they didn't have a problem with it.

Unfortunately, as much as I like military life, and as good as I believe the normal day-to-day life can be for a family, the life of deployment cannot be ignored. Many of my friends on active duty are on their third deployment in the last five years and, with John and me being dual military, I could not handle my daughter having that life. One of her parents would always be deployed; maybe both sometimes. She would have to go back and forth between living with one of us or our families. And that would provide no kind of stability for her. And that is unfair.

It was for this reason that John and I first chose to get out. For John, it was okay. He had a civilian mechanic job which he enjoyed, lived near his family, and didn't have to worry about 0600 hours PT. I, on the other hand, regretted the decision from the time I made it. There hasn't been a day that I woke up, after leaving the Army, that I didn't think about going back and wished that I had never got out. This is where the Guard came in.

When John and I got married, I made an agreement that, if he would marry me in Oregon, I would move back to Georgia. I had thought about going back to the Army myself so that we only had one parent in and didn't have to worry about both of us being deployed, but John would then be stuck following me around the world; having to get a job wherever I was stationed; and moving whenever I was assigned a new duty post; and I knew he didn't want that kind of life. So, instead, I joined the Tennessee National Guard.

I didn't know much about the Guard at first. Only that they were reservist and, as far as it's concerned in my book, that made them less of a soldier. They were weekend warriors, the guys who I had looked down on before. But I was dying to get back to wearing the uniform, so I enlisted. I was probably one of the easiest enlistments my recruiter ever had, too. I walked into his office, stayed for about fifteen minutes, asked about a half dozen (or less) questions, and came back the next day so he could swear me in.

At first, I refused to call myself Guard. When someone asked, I still said I was Army. I wanted to be back in the uniform and back in the military. But I had a hard time relating myself to these people who seemed to lack respect for regulations. They all called each other by their first names, seemed to have no concept of rank structure, and it was a week in there before I finally saw someone wear their head gear. Then, when I did, they had it on in the building. I know things like that may not seem like a big deal but, to me, they're just part of basic military bearing and I figured, if they couldn't wear their headgear properly, everything else was probably just as messed up.

It wasn't until a few weeks after I joined the Guard and left for recruiting school that I began to get a different opinion. Many of the people I met there had been in for a while. A good portion of them were active duty before they joined the Guard, and another good portion had all served in Iraq. Many of them had joined the Guard for the same reason I had. So that they may still have their normal lives back home, but serve their country at the same time.

The more Guardsmen I met, the more I began to figure out that a lot of my assumptions were wrong. Their laid back attitude that I had previously taken for a lack of military bearing was not that, but was the fact that many of them were so close and had relationships outside of the Guard. Unlike active duty, where you shipped to different bases around the world, your armory is often near your home. This leads to the unit being made up of people who have known each other since they were kids, people who work in there civilians jobs together and, often, even family members being a part of the same unit.

On the deployment I am currently on, there are a husband and a wife with us, a brother and a sister, two pairs of brothers, and a father and a son. In addition to that, many of the people who volunteered to go this time were the same people who deployed together last time and for other missions in years prior. They all have histories together and bonds outside of the military. It's this reason that they all call each other by first name, and that you will often see a private talking to a senior NCO as though they're friends, for they probably are.

The relationships don't make them any less of a soldier. We build the same bond and comradery on active duty. We are just introduced for the first time by last name, so that is how we come to know each other. My husband and I first met on active duty. I met him as Turnipseed, not as John. And, to this day, I have yet to call him by his first name in uniform. I had it explained to me by one Guardsman, on why they didn't care about names: they prefer to focus on what's important.

This difference in attitude isn't the only thing separating the Guard from the Army. Each one has its good and its bad points; its advantages and disadvantages over the other. One of the disadvantages was the promotion policies. Getting promoted can be like pulling teeth. People often have to jump around to different MOS's and companies to get promoted. The buddy system still has a lot to do with affecting the amount of promotion points you will get. And even a soldier who is a dirt bag has the possibility of getting promoted over the guy who is the high speed perfect solider if he chose the right job field.

The promotion problems are in the policy, though, not the individual companies. And, as far as the bad soldier getting promoted because he chose the right job, let's face it. It happens in the active Army just as much.

One of the benefits of the Guard, though, is the freedom which you have to attend schools and volunteer for missions. You can truly get everything that the military has to offer out of the Guard. In active duty, you normally have to be assigned to an airborne unit in order to go to airborne school, or reenlist for a new job. In the Guard, you just have to find a slot. The Guard offers all the same schools as the military and, for a soldier who is willing to work for them, they are often more likely to obtain admission. Missions are the same way. If another unit in the state is going to Egypt for a month or to Iraq for a year, you can volunteer to go with them. You can continue to volunteer with the same people you trusted from your last mission, or make a point to stay away from the ones you didn't.

Since I've been in, I've only been able to go to Katrina and Iraq. But other members I know have gone to Arizona for Border Patrol, deployed to Kosovo and Afghanistan, and gone to Egypt and Germany for training. The Guard seems to offer a wider variety of missions, whereas the active duty people I know just keep going back to Iraq over and over again.

It's also easier to move and live where you want. Since I joined the Guard in 2005, I've gone from the Tennessee National Guard, to the Oregon National Guard, on to Wyoming, and now I'm back in Tennessee. When I get home, it's quite possible that I may move to another state. And it will take no more effort than a phone call to a new unit to find a slot and notification to my current unit.

I still love the Army and miss the Army. There are still many days where I think about going back, mainly because I just want to be a full time soldier. Then I think about all that the Guard has to offer, how much further I can progress in my military career, and how much more I can get out of it, and I change my mind. There are still things about the Guard that still get to me, but I'm slowly learning to adjust. I may not yet be able to get myself to call my husband, who is in my unit, by his first name while in uniform, but I no longer get bothered when other people do.

# My Biggest Upset

BEFORE I WENT ON LEAVE, we had an incident with a man detainee. I won't go into too many specifics because, even though it is a past event, I don't want to write anything that may be considered a violation of operation security. The basics of it, though, are that a man was removed from another compound and sent to our compound because he feared for his life.

When the man got to the front gate of our compound, he refused to enter out of the same fear. We put him in a holding area to await the people we had that were in charge of things like interrogation and gathering information.

While we waited, I was placed as the guard over the detainee. He was an old man, very polite, and spoke some English. He tried to explain the situation to me, and I told him that he would have to wait until the other gentleman got there. When he did, I was there for the conversation. I overheard them talk, and listened as the individual got the detainee to agree to enter another portion of our compound, one that we knew was worse.

When he left, the interpreter and I looked at each

other and both said to each other "They're going to kill him." Everyone knew it. But there was nothing we could do. The person who made the decisions was a civilian and had access to information we didn't. We hoped that he knew something we didn't, and that he made the call for a reason. As we would come to find out the next day, we should have trusted our guts.

We didn't even make it until the next shift before we were being called in to search the compound. The other detainees had broken the arms and legs of the man whom we reassured would be okay. I went on leave, upset. All I could think about was that it could have been prevented if the civilian would have done his job. But it was 0100 when it happened, and I truly believe he just told the guy he would be okay so that he could go back to bed.

After I got back from leave, I found out that we had not only got a detainee injured, but had sentenced him to his death. The injuries he had sustained caused his death.

I never saw any torture, mistreatment, or violations of the Geneva code. Hell, I think the detainees got treated better than us most of the time. We got in trouble when we turned off their air conditioning after a riot. At the time, we didn't even have A/C. But, still, that one death was preventable, and it happened to a man because he tried to help us out. The idea that it was something I could have stopped, or at least could have tried to prevent, will bother me forever.

# Morale and Leadership

*To whom it may concern,*

*I have lost something from this deployment that I fear I may never regain. It's not my spouse, a loved one, my money, or even my dog. It's the sense of pride and the desire to serve that the Army has given me for so many years. Upon leaving home for this deployment, I would have sworn that, if you cut open my veins, I would bleed OD green. But since this deployment, everything has changed. I've seen where the military is going and what it will one day be and it scares me. It seems that our leadership has forgotten what it was like to be in our shoes, and fails to realize just how much we matter. Our leadership is responsible for both the mission and the morale of their troops.*

*The NCO creed reads "My two basic responsibilities will always be uppermost in my mind—accomplishment of my mission and the welfare of my Soldiers." Yet it is very rare that you see one concerned with either. More than once I have heard comments from higher ranking, that they didn't care about us and we didn't matter. I even once listened to a chaplain say I'll come back "when I have time to care." And now, nearing the end our deployment,*

125

*things have only begun to get worse.*

*We were just instructed that, for our awards ceremony, any individual not meeting height and weight will be required to stand behind the stage, for they are not to be seen during the ceremony. They were told that they could receive their awards when the ceremony is over. I am very big on enforcing the Army weight control program, but these individuals, which comprise probably 1/3 of our company, have served side by side with us for the entire deployment, and only now has there been a problem with it.*

*At some point, getting promoted changed from the pride in receiving the rank to being about the paycheck. I think it was about the same time we started referring to ourselves as "today's Army." I would like to remind our leadership that while we may be the future of the military, you will make us in your image. We will become what you make us. So please stop worrying about whether our pt belt is facing from left to right or right to left and take care of your soldiers. It is your lack of leadership that degrades our morale and hinders the mission. You are the sole reason for the Army's retention problem.*

*To my fellow soldiers who my battalion seeks to disgrace, I am proud to have served with you. You have taught me much, and I am honored to have known you. When the ceremony begins, I will make sure to be where I belong, next to the soldiers I have so proudly served with, behind the stage.*

*SPC Turnipseed*
*Camp Bucca, Iraq*

The previous letter is one that I wrote to Stars and Stripes, a paper we receive here in country. It printed a little bit different, an edited version, if you will. We've had a long year of stupidity and, only two weeks from returning home, they decided that they would increase it. I still love my country, and am proud to be a soldier, but after a year of hoping and planning to do my tour and then return to active duty, I have decided not to. I will still serve in the Guard, and hope to become an officer so that I may one day be able to improve the lives of my fellow soldiers. But I know that it will be a long time off until I will be in a position where I may be able to make an Impact.

I *can* say that this deployment has saddened me. It has soured the one thing that I loved so much. Whenever I met a person who had a bad outlook on the military, because they were at a bad duty station or in a bad company, I used to remind them that it's not all like that. But after being here, it seems like that is where it is all going.

I did a survey on leadership and morale, while I was here, for a college term paper I was writing. The topic of my paper was intended to be on the B Co. 1–181's degraded sense of morale while stationed at Camp Bucca, Iraq. I surveyed my company's current morale level compared to the morale level they had regarding the deployment, as well as their opinions on what was the main contributing factor in it. I was not at all surprised by the results of my company, but was surprised to find that the companies I had surveyed as a control group had the same opinions.

Nearly three-fourths of the people's morale had dropped significantly, and they all attributed it to leadership at their company level or higher. The only company I found that did not have the same response was a unit from Texas that currently had one of our Tennessee 1st sergeants in charge. In that company, not a single person complained about leadership. Many of them even saw it fit to tell me how much their morale had improved since he had been assigned to them. It was then when I saw just how much of an impact that leadership had on morale.

This particular 1SG was not known for being the buddy-buddy type. Truth is, he is a complete hard ass. Most people refer to him as a prick. And, if there is a conversation about him, it's usually not positive. But while we all complain about him, we also know that he will take care of us. When other companies were handing out article 15's (basically that's means getting written up) and taking soldiers' money, he would enforce extra duty. It may be humiliating to rake sand for three hours where everyone can see you, but I don't know a soul who wouldn't take it over losing $3,000 over the next three months; money that most of us need for our families.

Yes, in the Army if you mess up, they usually take your money. Wake up late or get in a fight, and you lose a half-month's pay for up to three months. In addition, they can take rank and extra duty.

It may sound like I'm complaining about Army polices, but I'm not. Hit your commander, brutally assault another soldier, go AWOL, do something like that, and you should lose your money and rank. But don't take a good soldier's money because he messed up. As little as we make, every dime usually counts to most families.

Policies like this are often manipulated. It's done by officers' own power trips, and the Sergeant Major who stands on top of the pods to catch guys walking to the bathroom at 0200 without their shirt tucked in. People like this are the problem with the Army. They are not worried about their troops; rather they are worried about themselves. They do not try to instill pride and esprit de corps; rather they want to instill fear and break people down so that it is easier to control them.

I heard it said, once, that a good leader is someone who will require you to go to hell with them and make you glad you're there. I believe this is true. Unfortunately, I have yet to meet that person.

# Five Years Later

IT'S BEEN FIVE YEARS SINCE the Iraq war
started. Five years since I first watched our unit
cross over the border on TV. Five years since I got
married. Five years since I first said good bye to my
husband. And five years since we thought this war
would only last six months.

I'm getting ready to go home now. Our dates
have been pushed back and changed a million times
in the last month. But, no matter what, we should
have no more then another week or two in country.
I'm looking forward to going home. To seeing my
family, kissing my husband, and squeezing my
daughter so hard she's going to pop. I'm looking
forward to wearing jeans, taking a bath, and
cooking in my own kitchen. What I'm not looking
forward to, though, is that the kiss I will get to give
my husband will be a goodbye kiss.

In August, we were released on a four day
pass, during which my husband took his leave from
his civilian job and met me in Hawaii for my sister's wedding. His leave was paid leave where he
had to work at the company to even accrue the time
off. In addition to that, he had drill two weekends
before he left and the weekend after he got back,

and then his two-week duty just before everything else. All his leave was either military leave, or accrued paid leave from the last eighteen months. But, as soon as he came back from the wedding and gave notice of the next drill, he found himself fired.

He was stunned, being that he had just got promoted and, even though there are laws to protect reservists from being discharged from work duty to military obligation, all a company has to do to get around it is state another reason for the discharge. He used to fight me tooth and nail about going back in the Army but, after that, he finally decided working in the civilian world just wasn't the same. He decided to transfer to the Active Army. He enlisted in April and, by May, was stationed in Fort Hood, Texas, once again. Upon arriving to his new unit, he found out that they had just recently deployed and that he would be going with them.

Since I first went to Iraq, the Army has changed the deployment policy back down to twelve months. But that doesn't come into effect until August. So my husband's unit will still be doing the fifteen month tour. Because he is arriving to his company after they left, he will be lucky enough to only have to serve about twelve months of it, but that is still another year gone. By this time next year, John and I will have been married for six years. And four of it will have been spent in country or gone on other military missions and training. The sad thing is that it's not over. I have four years left on this enlistment, but still plan on spending another twenty-three years in until I retire. I want to go to OCS and OBC to become an officer, which is thirty-two weeks of school. John wants to be a drill sergeant and then become a warrant officer. Depending on which presidential candidate gets elected this fall, we could both be looking at at least one more tour, if not two more tours, to Iraq, not including other countries.

But it's who we are. It's what we do and what makes us proud. We didn't even make it out of active duty eighteen months before both of us were back in the Guard. Now, three years later, I'm finishing a tour in Iraq and he's getting ready to embark on another one. I will miss him terribly. The day I found out, the thought of losing him again caused me to cry for nearly an hour. But I must honestly admit that, as bad as it sounds, when he originally told me he was deploying, my first thought was that he was going to have more deployments than me.

# Back in Fort Hood

WE GOT HOME JUST BEFORE Memorial Day weekend. We had to go through several out-processing stations in two different states, but we managed to get done on Sunday afternoon, so my husband was able to drive up to Tennessee and come get me.

He and Georgia pulled up to the barracks where I was sitting with all my bags and I ran around to Georgia's side of the car and peeked in the window where she couldn't see me and watched her look for me. Then I moved around in front of her view and saw her eyes light up when she saw me. I opened up the door and got her out and, as I picked her up, I heard her say, "Guess what, Mommy." I replied with, "What, Pun'k'in?" and she said, "I love you!" And then she gave me a big hug.

Just then, John had come around from the other side of the car and had his arms around both of us. Georgia kept hugging me, letting go, and then hugging me again. It took a good minute or two before I was able to adjust to having Georgia with me, and finally I leaned over and gave John a kiss.

We both looked at each other with the all too familiar *"What-do-I-do-now?"* look that we get every time one of us comes home. Not quite sure what the other one is thinking or feeling, but just glad that we're there and that we have each other back.

We only took a minute to load up my bags and get into the car and then we took off for Texas, where John had to be by 0600 the next morning for formation.

The drive home was as eventful as usual. We were making good time and just enjoying each other's company, when eventually we stopped talking and noticed that the tire was low. The valve stem had slipped open and it took a creative effort to repair it.

Amongst our various adventures across the country, we've almost always had problems. On the first trip we ever took to Georgia to meet John's family, we hit a gaping pot hole in the middle of a storm, knocked off the catalytic converter, and John had to get under the car and finish removing it in the middle of the storm. So, while John was frustrated about the tire, all I could think about during it was how good it felt to be back home.

The next morning, after getting home, he had to go to work. And, after that, we spent the next few days unpacking all the things he still had in boxes from the move. I hadn't lived in this house before. He had only just recently moved in himself. But being back in Killeen and at Fort Hood, where we had originally met, felt like home.

The town had grown and changed a lot while were we gone. Most of my friends were either out of the military or had changed duty stations. But I was still happy to be back where I felt I had belonged. I looked up the one person that was still stationed here, and he was leaving for Iraq in a less than a week. But we still got together for drinks and reminisced about the old days.

The individual was SSG Root, who had been both a NCO in my Motor Pool and my Rear Detachment OIC for the last half of the year I was in the active duty Army. He was one of a few NCOs who I have heavily respected in my military career. And being able to sit down with him reminded me a lot of why I was in the military and why I loved to serve.

He told me about the time he remembered first thinking that I was alright. We were in the motor pool and our drain was clogged to the point the motor pool floor was flooding. He looked down at the drain and I said he wasn't putting his hand in there and I told him to get out of my way and put my arm down in about three feet of sludge. He said he never wanted to work with females in the motor pool but, at that moment, he had decided I was alright with him. For once, my cocky attitude had seemed to earn me respect.

We talked about our last few years and about the Army. We talked about what was right with it and what was wrong. And he told me that he thought I would make a good officer; that I had been in long enough to see where it was going wrong but was still young enough to be able to achieve a rank to fix it. He told me that he thought that I was someone who could make a difference and that, if I ever made the rank of Colonel, he would be there to pin me.

I had spent my whole deployment trying to decide if I should stay in the Guard and trying to find a civilian career that I liked or go back into the Army. But that night made up my mind. I've spent the last four years wishing I was back in active duty and, no matter how much I tried to find something else that would make me happy, I never would. I'm a soldier, and nothing I do will change that. I love who I am and what I do. It makes me proud of who I am and makes me feel like I'm a part of something greater then myself. I can credit the Army for almost everything that I am and have become. I love it and I truly can't imagine doing anything else.

# To be Continued...

OVER THIS LAST YEAR, I have worked very hard to complete my schooling. I am now in my last term before I graduate with my bachelor's degree in business, and have begun to look at master's programs. I would like to become an officer, but have begun to realize that I need to look outside the military if I ever truly hope to make an impact.

I have always been interested in business and management but, over the last year, I developed an increasing interest in foreign relations and public policy. A good friend who I met on this deployment constantly talked about how he would like to be a politician and make public service, once again, really be about serving the public. We began an on-going joke about racing each other to senator.

I still have a long road ahead of me in the military. In addition to becoming an officer, I would first like to make sergeant and, next year, I would like to compete in the German Armed Forces Badge for Military Proficiency. When John gets back from this deployment, it should be my turn to go again. And I'm hoping, at least this time, I will be able to go to another country, maybe something with vegetation.

We are planning and hoping that we will be able to have another child. Right now, this decision is our hardest. We want desperately to be able to give our daughter a sibling, and I know my husband would very much like a son. Our biggest controversy over this, though, is that we may bring another child into the world who is forced to deal with the absence of their parents. In all reality, we must first be able to remain in the same country long enough for this to even be an option. So, while it's something we talk about, it's not something that is likely in our future.

More than anything, I hope that my daughter will be able to understand everything that has happened when she gets older. She has done better than any child I have ever met when it comes to us being gone. I talked to her the other day about John leaving and her only response was, "You can come watch me." She seems to be fine, knowing that she will always have one of us. My biggest fear is that the day will come when both our units' deployments occur during the same period of time and we are both forced to leave her.

I can only hope that she knows that her parents love her and we didn't want to leave her. I hope she knows that, when we did, we did it for her, for her future, and the future of her country.

I have put in my release for active duty and hope to have it approved soon.

John has also seemed to have found his motivation and drive for the military again. He kept talking about all the different courses and schools he wants to attend; he's begun to work on his correspondence courses and even wants to finish his degree. We have a long road ahead of us as soldiers, as a couple, and as a family, but, with the military as our future, we both know that everything will work out and that, finally, we will be doing something with our lives.

The military is who we are. As Georgia said one day, "There's only one job in this house...that's the Army."

Printed in the United States
141373LV00002B/3/P